WALKS INTO HISTORY
LANCASHIRE

*Other titles from Countryside Books
covering Lancashire include:*

PUB WALKS IN LANCASHIRE
Alan Shepley

PUB WALKS FOR MOTORISTS: LANCASHIRE AND GT MANCHESTER
Nick Burton

VILLAGE WALKS IN LANCASHIRE
Nick Burton

LANCASHIRE TEASHOP WALKS
Jean Patefield

THOSE WERE THE DAYS: LANCASHIRE
Ron Freethy

LANCASHIRE 1939–1945: THE SECRET WAR
Ron Freethy

LANKIE TWANG
Ron Freethy

LANCASHIRE TALES OF MYSTERY & MURDER
Steve Fielding

LANCASHIRE WITHIN LIVING MEMORY
Lancashire Federation of Women's Institutes

LANCASHIRE AIRFIELDS IN THE SECOND WORLD WAR
Aldon P. Ferguson

LOST RAILWAYS OF LANCASHIRE
Gordon Suggitt

WALKS INTO HISTORY
LANCASHIRE

Brian Conduit

COUNTRYSIDE BOOKS
NEWBURY BERKSHIRE

First published 2006
© Brian Conduit 2006

COUNTRYSIDE BOOKS
3 Catherine Road
Newbury, Berkshire

To view our complete range of books,
please visit us at
www.countrysidebooks.co.uk

ISBN 1 85306 971 X
EAN 978 1 85306 971 0

Designed by Peter Davies, Nautilus Design

Produced through MRM Associates Ltd., Reading
Typeset by Techniset Typesetters, Newton-le-Willows
Printed by Woolnough Bookbinding Ltd., Irthlingborough

Contents

INTRODUCTION   8

WALK

1 RIBCHESTER FORT AND THE ROMAN CONQUEST OF BRITAIN
(5½ *miles*)   9

2 BLACKSTONE EDGE AND ROMAN TRANSPORT *(6 miles)*   15

3 CLITHEROE CASTLE AND THE MEDIEVAL BARONS *(7 miles)*   20

4 TURTON TOWER AND THE THREAT OF SCOTTISH INVASION
(6 miles)   25

5 WHALLEY ABBEY AND THE DISSOLUTION OF THE MONASTERIES
(5½ *miles*)   30

6 STONYHURST AND CATHOLIC PERSECUTION *(7½ miles)*   36

7 HOGHTON TOWER AND THE UNION OF THE ENGLISH AND
SCOTTISH CROWNS *(3½ miles)*   42

8 PENDLE HILL AND 17TH-CENTURY WITCHCRAFT *(6 miles)*   47

9 LANCASTER AND TRADE WITH THE AMERICAS *(6½ miles)*   52

10 WYCOLLER AND THE EARLY TEXTILE INDUSTRY
(8 or 6 miles)   58

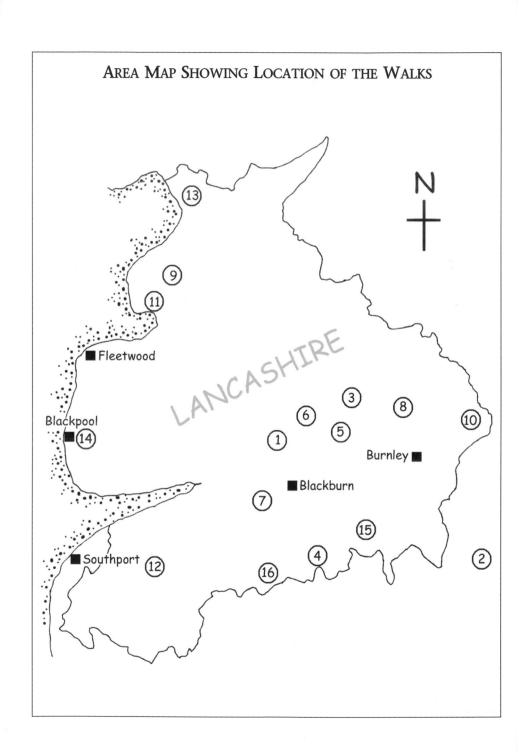

AREA MAP SHOWING LOCATION OF THE WALKS

WALK

11 GLASSON DOCK AND THE CANAL AGE *(8½ miles)*   64

12 RUFFORD OLD HALL AND THE AGRICULTURAL REVOLUTION
(5½ miles)   70

13 LEIGHTON HALL AND THE ENGLISH COUNTRY HOUSE
(6 miles)   75

14 BLACKPOOL TOWER AND THE VICTORIAN SEASIDE RESORT
(8 miles)   80

15 HELMSHORE TEXTILE MUSEUMS AND 'KING COTTON'
(5½ miles)   86

16 RIVINGTON AND A VICTORIAN PHILANTHROPIST *(5 miles)*   91

PUBLISHER'S NOTE

We hope that you obtain considerable enjoyment from this book; great care has been taken in its preparation. Although at the time of publication all routes followed public rights of way or permitted paths, diversion orders can be made and permissions withdrawn.

We cannot, of course, be held responsible for such diversion orders and any inaccuracies in the text which result from these or any other changes to the routes nor for any damage which might result from walkers trespassing on private property. We are anxious though that all details covering the walks are kept up to date and would therefore welcome information from readers which would be relevant to future editions.

The simple sketch maps that accompany the walks in this book are based on notes made by the author whilst checking out the routes on the ground. However, for the benefit of a proper map, we do recommend that you purchase the relevant Ordnance Survey sheet covering your walk. The Ordnance Survey maps are widely available, especially through booksellers and local newsagents.

INTRODUCTION

There is a lot of history in Lancashire. There is also an infinite variety of terrain. Put those two together and you have the ingredients for a series of highly attractive and fascinating walks.

Almost every walk in Britain is a walk through history. Evidence of the past is all around us and nobody on this island lives too far away from a historic site, whether it is a Roman fort, a medieval church, the ruins of an old castle, a great house or a Victorian industrial monument. Even some of the paths we tread have been in existence for hundreds of years.

Combining walking with visiting and understanding some of the monuments to our history is both worthwhile and fun. It gives an extra dimension to a stroll in the countryside and makes it more enjoyable. We can better appreciate a historic building by approaching it on foot, initially seeing it from a distance and relating it to its geographical setting.

As both an urban/industrial and rural/agricultural county, Lancashire's historic sites range from Roman and medieval remains to Tudor manor houses and the great monuments of the Industrial Revolution era when the Lancashire cotton industry was at its zenith. Few other counties can match its diversity of landscapes. These embrace the tree-fringed shorelines of Morecambe Bay, the rugged uplands of the Forest of Bowland, the lush valleys of the Lune and Ribble, the bare moorlands of the West and South Pennines and the flat former marshlands of the Fylde and West Lancashire.

The following routes introduce you to some of the major sites and buildings that illustrate Lancashire's past. I hope that you get enjoyment both from the different and varied landscapes through which they pass and from the historic places that are seen along the way.

Walking through history is very rewarding. It brings to life lessons at school, or what you have read in books or what you may have seen in television documentaries. As well as getting fresh air and exercise, an additional bonus is that you can combine it with good food and drink at the many welcoming pubs, restaurants and tea and coffee shops that are scattered in abundance throughout Lancashire.

Brian Conduit

Walk 1
Ribchester Fort and the Roman Conquest of Britain

Length: 5½ miles

The bath house at Ribchester. The floor supports, or Pilae, *for the underfloor heating system for the baths still remain.*

HOW TO GET THERE: Ribchester is on the B6245 about 7 miles north of Blackburn.

PARKING: In the pay-and-display car park at Ribchester.

MAP: OS Explorer 287 (West Pennine Moors) GR 650353.

Introduction

There are fine views throughout this circuit, especially towards the end when pleasant riverside walking is accompanied by magnificent views of the Ribble valley and Pendle Hill. The route includes all the Roman sites at Ribchester – the fort that once protected Roman Britain from the warlike tribes of the North, the bath house, and a museum – and also passes the interesting group of buildings at Stydd which date from a later time when the Knights Hospitallers of St John had a monastery here.

HISTORICAL BACKGROUND

Julius Caesar led the first Roman invasions of Britain in 55 and 54 BC but these were little more than brief raids. In 55 BC the Roman army hardly penetrated inland from the Kent coast. The second invasion a year later was a lengthier affair and, on this occasion, the invaders crossed the Thames and reached about as far as Hertfordshire.

The actual conquest, ordered by Emperor Claudius, began nearly a century later in 43 AD. Throughout that century, commercial ties between Britain and the Roman province of Gaul increased and there was evidence that the Britons were aiding the Gauls in their resistance to the Romans. This was the background to the imperial decision to launch an invasion and conquest of Britain.

From Kent, the Romans made their way northwards and westwards, crossing the Medway and reaching the banks of the Thames near the site of modern London. From there the army split into three groups: one advanced into the south-west, one marched across the Midlands to Wales and the third headed northwards into the wilder country of northern England and on towards Scotland. Despite much brave and spirited resistance, the advance was relatively easy, aided by divisions amongst the British tribes and the willingness of several tribal chiefs to co-operate with the invaders.

The revolt of the Iceni in East Anglia in 61 AD, led by their queen Boudicca, and the fiercer resistance that the invaders encountered the further north and west

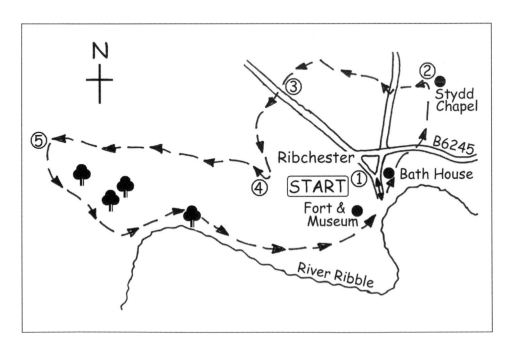

they went, slowed down this relentless advance for a time. However, the Iceni revolt was savagely suppressed and, under the energetic leadership of Agricola, Roman governor of Britain, the conquest continued into Wales, through northern England and on into Scotland.

The 73-mile long Hadrian's Wall, stretching across northern England from the mouth of the Tyne to the Solway, was built around 122 AD to establish the northern frontier of the Roman province of Britain. Scotland was considered too difficult and inhospitable to conquer and, from an economic point of view, not worth incorporating within the empire. The frontier was temporarily pushed further north into southern Scotland to the line of the Forth and Clyde, where the Antonine Wall – a turf construction – was built, but the Romans later fell back to Hadrian's Wall.

As they advanced the Romans established towns and villas, built forts and created a network of roads to link all parts of the province, but both geographically and culturally, Roman Britain became divided into two distinct areas. There was a civil zone in the more settled, drier and warmer south and east and this was where almost all the villas and civilian towns were established. The wilder, colder and more warlike north and west was a military zone and it was here that the Romans built most of their forts and stationed the bulk of their armed forces. Ribchester was one of a chain of forts that were constructed all over northern England.

THE WALK

❶ Turn left out of the car park to a T-junction and turn right through the village to the river.

From here, the view upstream of the great bend in the Ribble, backed by the distinctive outline of Pendle Hill, is especially memorable.

Turn left along the tarmac riverside path, signposted to the Roman Bath House, and the path curves left away from the river to continue beside a stream, passing the sparse remains of the bath house.

The bath house was part of the vicus, or civilian settlement, that grew up outside the walls of the fort. It appears to have been in use between about AD 100 and 225 and was frequented by civilians as well as soldiers. It is a good illustration of how sophisticated life was for the average Roman soldier, even when stationed in a relatively wild and remote part of the empire as Ribchester. The site has never been fully excavated as part of it lies under the adjacent school and playground.

There is no admission charge and the bath house is usually open every day between Easter and October.

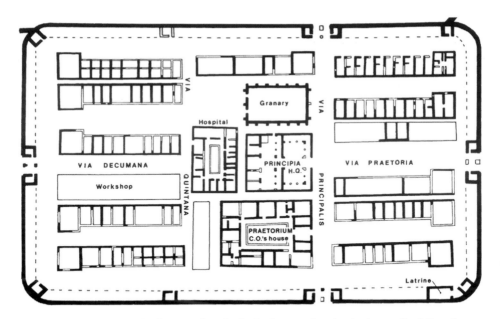

No Roman fort was exactly the same, but the basic shape and main streets usually followed a standard pattern. This is Housesteads on Hadrian's Wall, one of the best preserved Roman forts in Britain.

At a Ribble Way sign, turn right onto a path which curves left across a grassy area to a road and turn right to a T-junction. Turn right in front of the Ribchester Arms and turn left along a tarmac track called Stydd Lane. The route passes, in turn, the Catholic church, Stydd almshouses and Stydd chapel.

This is an interesting and varied group of buildings and they all lie within a short distance of each other. The first is the Catholic church which dates from 1789. It was a 'barn church', built so as to disguise the fact that it was used for worship. At the time English Catholics were not legally allowed to have their own churches.

Just ahead are the early 18th-century almshouses, a most attractive and dignified architectural composition. They were built by the Shireburn family from nearby Stonyhurst, to house five poor people.

Finally – just beyond where the route turns left – there is Stydd chapel. This small church is all that remains of a monastery belonging to the Knights Hospitallers of St John of Jerusalem. The knights were a crusading order, founded in 1113 in order to provide protection and assistance for pilgrims to the Holy Land, and they had a number of small monasteries, called commanderies, scattered throughout England. By the time of the dissolution of the monasteries in the 1530s, there were only fifteen left. Stydd was dissolved around the middle of the 14th century.

❷ In front of the chapel, turn left down an embankment and walk across a field to a footbridge. Cross it and the path curves right to a stile. Climb this, walk across a field, go over another stile and continue along a paved enclosed path. Climb a stile, keep ahead and climb one more stile onto a road.

Turn left and at a 30 mph sign, turn sharp right along a tarmac track towards a farm. Walk through the farmyard, continue along the track and climb a stile to the right of a gate. Turn right, left and left again around a small enclosure to return to the track and keep ahead along another track which descends, crosses a stream and then ascends to a road.

❸ Take the track ahead through a farmyard and continue downhill to a gate. Go through, keep ahead along the right edge of a field and immediately after passing through a gap into the next field, bear left and head downhill to a footbridge. Cross it, keep ahead to climb a stile, bear left and continue uphill across a field, making for the top left-hand corner.

❹ In the corner, turn sharp right to keep along the left field edge and just before reaching the next corner, bear slightly right to a gate. Go through and walk across the next field to a waymarked gate in the far left corner. After going through it, continue along an enclosed track, go through another gate and head straight across the next field, passing to the left of a tree-enclosed pool. Do not continue to a waymarked footbridge but bear left and descend to a metal gate. Go through, keep ahead along the right field edge, above a stream, climb a stile, continue across the next field and go through a gate on the far side. Keep along the right edge of a field and go through a gate onto a tarmac track.

❺ Turn left and where the tarmac ends, keep ahead along a fence-lined track to a gate. Go through, head gently downhill across a field, making for a gate, go through that one and continue downhill.

For the remainder of the walk there is a series of splendid views over the Ribble valley.

At the bottom of the field, turn left along a track which descends towards farm buildings. Go through a gate and turn left along a tarmac track which winds downhill to a gate. Go through it and another gate ahead and continue along a fence-lined track. Where this track curves left, turn right over a ladder stile and head up over the shoulder of a hill.

Continue above the river and, following the edge of the trees on the right, descend quite steeply to a stile. After climbing it, walk across riverside meadows to a kissing gate, go through and continue along an enclosed track back to Ribchester.

The Roman fort at Ribchester (Latin name Bremetennacum) was established around 78 AD and was situated in the heart of territory occupied by the warlike Brigantes tribe. Originally built in turf and timber, it was later rebuilt mainly in stone soon after 100 AD.

Ribchester occupied an important strategic position at a crossing point on the River Ribble and at the crossroads of the north-south route from Manchester to Hadrian's Wall and the east-west route from Kirkham to Ilkley and York. Most of the site remains unexcavated as part lies under the churchyard and the south-eastern corner is now covered by the Ribble as the river has changed its course since Roman times. The fort was in use for around 300 years and accommodated approximately 500 cavalry soldiers, most of who came from modern Spain and Hungary.

It had the usual playing card shape, common to most Roman forts throughout the empire, but the only part still visible above ground is the granary, with its hypocaust or central heating system, located at the side of the churchyard. As compensation for the lack of buildings, the splendid museum on the site has some fine displays, houses many of the objects excavated from the fort and provides detailed information on the history of Roman Britain and the Roman Empire as a whole.

For details of opening times and admission charges, telephone 01254 878261.

> ### REFRESHMENTS
>
> The White Bull in Ribchester is a historic building in itself. Dating from the early 18th century, it has beamed bar areas, the garden overlooks the Roman bath house and the columns supporting the portico at the front are alleged to be from the Roman fort, dug up from the Ribble. It serves a wide variety of meals, from soup and sandwiches to a Sunday roast (telephone: 01254 878303). There are also other pubs and a café in Ribchester.

After passing the museum, follow the road as it bends left through the village to return to the start.

WALK 2

BLACKSTONE EDGE AND ROMAN TRANSPORT

Length: 6 miles

The Roman road on Blackstone Edge – still as it was laid some 2,000 years ago.

HOW TO GET THERE: To reach the start of the walk at Hollingworth Lake Country Park Visitor Centre, take the B6225 from the centre of Littleborough, turn left at the lakeshore by the Fisherman's Inn and turn left again.

PARKING: In the pay-and-display car park at Hollingworth Lake Country Park.

MAP: OS Outdoor Leisure 21 (South Pennines) GR 939153.

INTRODUCTION

The pleasant, undulating and well-wooded country around Hollingworth Lake near the start and finish of the walk is in complete contrast to the bare and windswept surroundings of the Roman road as it climbs onto Blackstone Edge. From here the impressive and extensive views take in a wide swathe of bleak Pennine moorland, and look towards Rochdale and Manchester.

HISTORICAL BACKGROUND

The majority of motorists probably do not realise when driving along many of our modern major highways that they are following the line of a Roman road. Much of the A1 keeps to the route of Ermine Street, the Roman road from London to the north. The A5 follows the line of Watling Street which ran from London to the Midlands and the North-West, and when travelling between Exeter and Lincoln, much of the way you will be driving along the old Fosse Way. Although some trackways existed in prehistoric times, the Romans were the first road builders in Britain. So well were they constructed that stretches of paved Roman roadway still survive after nearly 2,000 years of neglect, vandalism and the British weather.

As the principal city of Roman Britain, London was then, as now, the hub of the road system. The roads were the chief means of communication and were constructed all over the country to link the main centres of population – civil and military – as quickly and efficiently as possible. It was not an easy task. The Roman engineers experienced similar difficulties to those faced by British colonialists when building railways in 19th-century Africa, through thickly forested territory populated by hostile or, at least, unwelcoming tribes.

Initially, the main purposes of the roads were military and political; to enable soldiers to move quickly to real or potential trouble spots and to allow government officials to go about their business administering this distant province of Rome's vast empire. Later, as the province became more settled and

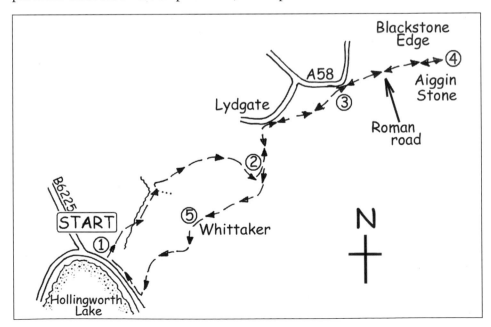

peaceful, they became major commercial arteries and trade flowed along them, to and from the main ports and between the main towns and forts. Generally they were built in a straight line but where this was not possible, they followed the natural contours of the land, taking the easiest and most logical route.

After the Romans abandoned Britain in the early 5th century, it seems inconceivable that their roads did not continue to be used but, inevitably, lack of maintenance and general neglect caused them to deteriorate over time. It was not until the Industrial Revolution thirteen centuries later that Britain was to have anything like a comparable road-building programme.

THE WALK

Hollingworth Lake was originally constructed in the early 19th century as a feeder reservoir for the Rochdale Canal. In Victorian times it became a popular resort for the workers of Rochdale, Oldham and other local towns and was nicknamed 'The Weighvers Seaport'. Thousands flocked here at weekends and bank holidays and there were pubs, cafés, dance halls, funfairs, rowing and boating trips across the lake on a steam ferry.

❶ Facing the visitor centre, turn right along a track and go through a gate. Continue along the track and where it bends right, turn left along a path through a picnic area. After crossing a footbridge over a stream, turn left, go through a gate and continue along an attractive path by the stream on the left. Keep ahead, going through a succession of gates, to reach a T-junction. Turn left along a tarmac track, still with the stream on the left, and look out for where you turn sharp right up steps to a kissing gate. Go through, keep ahead and turn left in front of a gate. Cross a footbridge, continue gently uphill above a stream on the left and go through a kissing gate to emerge onto the edge of Whittaker golf course. The route across it is well signed and you soon join a track that leads to a gate. Go through and keep ahead along the track to meet a tarmac path.

❷ Continue along it to the hamlet of Lydgate and just before emerging onto a road, turn right along a track, passing in front of a row of cottages. This is the start of the ascent of Blackstone Edge. Head steadily uphill by a wall on the right, bearing left away from the wall to reach a tarmac track.

❸ Turn right and where the track bears right, keep ahead along a rough grassy path, rejoining a wall on the right. As you climb, the stones of the Roman road appear and become more impressive the higher you get, especially after crossing a drainage channel.

This well-preserved stretch of paved Roman road rises steeply out of Littleborough at gradients of up to 1 in 4, to cross the Pennines at Blackstone Edge. There have always

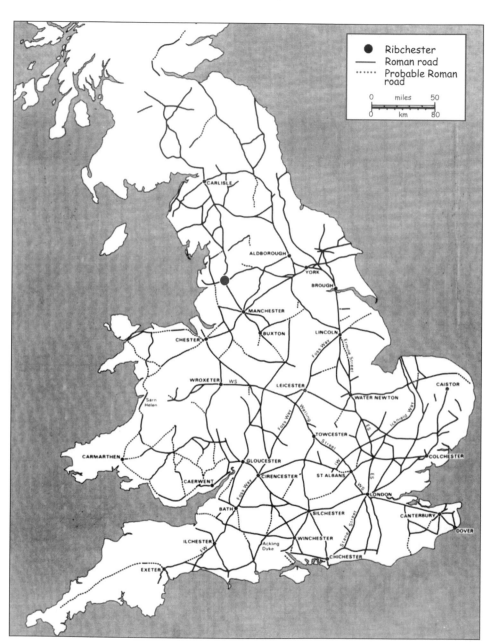

The main road network at the time of Roman Britain.

been some niggling doubts as to whether it is Roman at all. Some historians have put forward a later date, suggesting that it may be a medieval road, but it is always referred to as the Roman road and is named as such on Ordnance Survey maps. Furthermore, its location fits in with the likely line of a trans-Pennine route between the Roman forts of Mamucium (Manchester) and Olicana (Ilkley).

Whatever its origins, it is regarded as one of the most impressive stretches of surviving ancient roadway in the country. The stone setts and kerbs, resting on a foundation of sand and rubble, are clearly exposed – looking almost as good as new – and the ditches at the side, constructed for drainage, can be seen. The middle trough is an interesting feature not usually seen on other stretches of Roman road. It was probably intended for braking purposes; the brake pole of the cart would be inserted into the groove to reduce the speed on the steep descent.

Continue up as far as the Aiggin Stone near the top where the Pennine Way crosses the road.

The Aiggin Stone is thought to be around 600 years old. It was probably a guide stone, put here to help medieval travellers find their way across the open and featureless moorland.

❹ Retrace your steps downhill to where you joined the tarmac track near Lydgate (2) and continue along it. At a fork, take the right-hand tarmac track and pass the golf club entrance to reach the secluded hamlet of Whittaker.

❺ Bear right between houses, go through a wall gap and follow a slabbed path which bends left to go through another wall gap. Continue along an enclosed path, go through a gate and head downhill through Whittaker Wood to a gate at the bottom. Go through, turn right, continue downhill and cross a footbridge over a stream. Now head uphill to a waymarked post and continue to a gate by a public footpath sign. Go through, keep ahead alongside a fence bordering a drain on the left and, after going through a kissing gate, continue along a raised embankment above the drain. Climb two stiles in quick succession and turn left over the drain. Turn right and continue along the other side of the drain, heading up to go through a gate. Keep ahead along a path to a tarmac track, turn right downhill to a road and continue along it beside Hollingworth Lake. Take the first turning on the right to return to the visitor centre.

WALK 3

CLITHEROE CASTLE AND THE MEDIEVAL BARONS

Length: 7 miles

The 12th-century keep of Clitheroe Castle.

HOW TO GET THERE: The walk starts in the Market Place at Clitheroe, which is situated north-east of Blackburn.

PARKING: There are plenty of pay-and-display car parks in Clitheroe.

MAP: OS Explorer OL 41 (Forest of Bowland & Ribblesdale) GR 744419.

INTRODUCTION

There are splendid views throughout this walk, especially of Clitheroe Castle, Pendle Hill and across the Ribble valley to the line of the Bowland Fells. Although Clitheroe Castle has one of the smallest Norman keeps in the country, it dominates the town and can be seen from many vantage points throughout the surrounding countryside. On the latter part of the route there is also pleasant walking beside the Ribble. There may be some muddy stretches in places, especially when near farms.

HISTORICAL BACKGROUND

Throughout the Middle Ages, the barons were a constant problem for English kings and keeping them in check and curbing their power was an issue that transcended all others. There were numerous baronial rebellions during which kings were humiliated, several lost their thrones and some even lost their lives.

The vast majority of the barons owed their land and wealth to William the Conqueror's victory at the battle of Hastings in 1066. William rewarded those

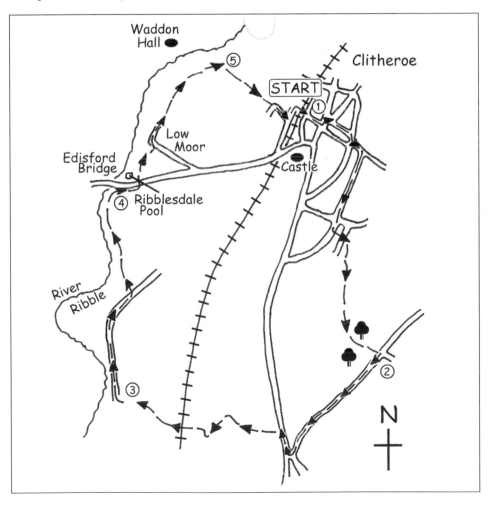

who had accompanied him on the invasion of England and helped him win the English throne by granting them the lands of the dispossessed Saxon landowners. Although subject to the king, the baronial estates were virtual kingdoms in which the barons had almost complete power. Their armies were raised on behalf of the king and at the king's request but these armies could easily be turned against the king, as well as against each other in disputes over power and land.

One check that the king had over the barons was that they did not hold their lands in one compact block but generally had them scattered throughout the country. Exceptions were those who held land on the Welsh and Scottish borders. Here the dangers to England's security meant that the barons were given almost regal powers in return for defending those borders on behalf of the king.

The power of the barons was only broken by the accession of Henry VII, first of the powerful Tudor monarchs, in 1485. Several factors contributed to this. The long Wars of the Roses (1455-85), basically a baronial struggle for the throne of England, had weakened the barons, both militarily and financially. The changing nature of warfare, particularly the introduction of gunpowder, meant that their castles were becoming obsolete and no longer able to withstand attacks. By the middle of the 16th century, too, the monarchy had become stronger and wealthier as a result of Henry VIII making himself head of the Church and seizing the lands and possessions of the monasteries.

THE WALK

Clitheroe Castle was built around 1186 by Robert de Lacy. The De Lacys were powerful landowners and the castle was the administrative and military centre of their large estates in the locality, known as the Honour of Clitheroe.

In the early 14th century, Clitheroe Castle passed through inheritance to the Earls of Lancaster but, after the execution of the second earl in 1322 for taking part in a rebellion against Edward II, the castle and its estates were forfeited to the Crown. Throughout its history the castle saw little action and by the Tudor period had fallen into decay. During the Civil War, it was captured by Royalist troops in 1644 but soon surrendered to the forces of Parliament. Afterwards Clitheroe suffered the fate of most castles in Britain; Cromwell's government ordered it to be slighted (i.e. destroyed) to the extent that it could not be used for military purposes again.

Among the medieval owners of Clitheroe Castle, Henry de Lacy (1251-1311) was probably the most powerful. He was Earl of Lincoln and Lord of Denbigh and, as well as possessing Clitheroe Castle and extensive property in Lancashire around Clitheroe and Blackburn, he owned castles and vast estates around Pontefract in Yorkshire and Denbigh in North Wales. He also had a residence in London. His record was an exemplary one of service and loyalty to the monarchy. As a soldier, he fought in wars in Wales, Scotland and France and he also served the Crown as a statesman and diplomat. He enclosed part of his estates in Rossendale to construct a deer park and was responsible for helping the monks of Stanlaw move to Whalley.

One of the later owners of Clitheroe Castle, Thomas, Earl of Lancaster, illustrates the other side of baronial conduct. For taking part in a rebellion against Edward II in 1322, he was executed and his lands were forfeited to the Crown. They remained part of the royal estates until the 17th century.

Of the medieval castle, there is little left apart from the 12th-century keep. The other buildings are mainly 18th-century reconstructions, possibly incorporating former castle buildings. One of them houses an interesting museum (fee payable) in which the various exhibits depict the story of the castle and the archaeology and social history of Clitheroe and the Ribble valley.

The castle keep is open every day between dawn and dusk and admission is free. For details of opening times telephone 01200 424635.

❶ Facing the library, turn right down Wellgate and continue down Shawbridge Street to a main road (A671). Cross over, take the road opposite (still Shawbridge Street) and take the third road on the right, Hayhurst Street, which later becomes Littlemoor Road. After ½ mile – and shortly after passing Peel Park Avenue – turn left at a public footpath sign to Pendleton, onto an enclosed path which emerges onto a road. Turn right and turn left onto an enclosed path at another public footpath sign. The path keeps along the edge of a playing field, bearing right and later bending left to reach a kissing gate. Go through, walk across a field, cross a footbridge and continue across the next field. Descend alongside a wall on the left to cross a stream, continue by the wall, go through a kissing gate and walk along a track which bends left to reach a lane.

❷ Turn right along it for about ¾ mile, eventually going through a gate onto a road. Turn right and at a public footpath sign, turn left over a ladder stile. Head across a field, climb a stile, continue along the right edge of the next field and climb a stile in the corner. Turn left along a tarmac track and where this track curves right, keep ahead through a kissing gate and walk across a farmyard. Keep to the left of a barn, turn right at the corner of the barn and go through a kissing gate onto a track. Immediately turn right through another gate and at a yellow waymark, turn left over a stile and walk along an enclosed path, descending gently to cross a footbridge over a railway line.

Ahead there are attractive views over the Ribble Valley to Kemple End and both Mitton church and Stonyhurst College are clearly visible.

After a choice between a stile and a kissing gate, the way continues along the right edge of a new plantation, Standen Hey Community Woodland. Climb a stile in the corner and bear right across the next field, making for a gate in the right-hand corner. Go through it to pick up a track which leads to another gate, go through that one, keep ahead and pass to the left of farm buildings to reach a lane.

❸ Turn right, here joining the Ribble Way, and follow this lane, initially beside the Ribble, for just over ½ mile. Just after crossing a stream, turn left

along a track, at public footpath and Ribble Way signs, turn right onto another track and go through a kissing gate. Head diagonally across a field. Go through a gate and the path descends through trees to the riverbank. Go through a kissing gate and walk beside the river, passing through another kissing gate, to Edisford Bridge.

❹ In front of the bridge, bear right up to the road and turn left along the drive to Ribblesdale Pool. At the end of the drive, keep ahead across grass to a Ribble Way post and turn right along the left edge of a playing field. At the next Ribble Way post, bear right across the corner of the field and pass in front of houses to a road at Low Moor.

The grid pattern of the older parts of Low Moor indicates that it was a planned industrial community based around the now vanished cotton mill. Clitheroe was on the northern edge of the Lancashire cotton belt. The mill, an enormous building on the banks of the Ribble, was founded in 1782, enlarged in 1799 and finally demolished in 1967. Its site is now occupied by a modern housing estate. Low Moor church, built between 1867 and 1869, is a fine example of the Victorian Gothic style.

Turn left, immediately turn right and at a fork, take the right-hand road which becomes a track. Keep along it to a Ribble Way sign where you go through a kissing gate. Bear right up to a footpath post and keep beside a fence on the right above the river.

❺ At the next footpath post – just before reaching the top of some steps – turn right and head across a field to a kissing gate in the corner. Go through, walk along a left field edge to a pair of kissing gates, go through the right-hand one and continue across the next field to another kissing gate. After going through it, walk across a field and climb a stile onto a lane. Turn left along Back Commons and turn right into Kirkmoor Road. At a T-junction, turn left to Clitheroe railway station. Walk along a tarmac path between the station and houses and turn right under a railway bridge. Turn right again, turn left and follow the road uphill to a crossroads. Turn right for the entrance to the castle; the starting point is just to the left.

WALK 4

TURTON TOWER AND THE THREAT OF SCOTTISH INVASION

Length: 6 miles

Turton Tower.

HOW TO GET THERE: Batridge Barn car park at Entwhistle Reservoir is signposted from the B6391 between Darwen and Chapeltown.

PARKING: Batridge Barn car park.

MAP: OS Explorer 287 (West Pennine Moors) GR 723173.

INTRODUCTION

This walk across open moorland, through woodland and beside three scenic reservoirs has a host of extensive views. At times, the monument to Sir Robert Peel on Holcombe Moor can be seen and the spire of Chapeltown church is visible for much of the route. Turton Tower, a pele tower built in the 15th century for protection against Scottish raiders, is the major focal point but additional interest is provided by the battlemented railway bridge and impressive Victorian viaduct.

HISTORICAL BACKGROUND

Warfare between England and Scotland was an almost permanent feature of British history throughout the Middle Ages and on into the 16th century. It only

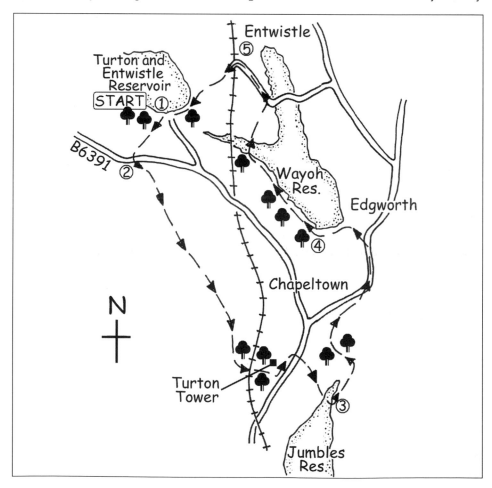

declined after the union of the crowns when James VI of Scotland became James I of England and Wales in 1603 and did not entirely die out until after the crushing of the Jacobite uprising at the Battle of Culloden in 1746. Moreover, even when the two kingdoms were not at war with each other, skirmishes and raids across the border continued.

The wars arose out of the claim of the English kings to be overlords of Scotland, which was naturally disputed by the Scottish kings, and disputes over where the border should run. After several centuries of relative calm and stability, relations between the two countries worsened following the death of Alexander III of Scotland in 1286. His successor was his young granddaughter Margaret, the Maid of Norway, but she died in a shipwreck while on her way to Scotland in 1290. The lack of a clear successor and the competing claims of several candidates gave the ambitious English King Edward I, fresh from his successful conquest of Wales, the ideal opportunity to intervene as umpire in the question of the Scottish succession. He chose John Balliol, in the expectation that Balliol would be his puppet, but this inevitably provoked Scottish resistance. Initially this resistance was led by William Wallace and, after Wallace's defeat at Falkirk in 1298, by the new Scottish king, Robert Bruce.

Edward I died in 1307 while on his way to Scotland to deal with Bruce. The crushing defeat of his son, Edward II, at Bannockburn in 1314 secured Scotland's independence but this only increased the irregular warfare waged by the powerful barons on both sides of the border. Throughout the 14th, 15th and 16th centuries, the history of the borders was mainly one long and vicious story of raids, killings and destruction of property. Although the border counties of Cumberland and Westmorland suffered the most, Scottish raids did extend into north Lancashire, reaching on some occasions as far south as the Ribble.

The larger and more powerful landowners had their great castles from which to launch attacks and to defend themselves but, because of the frequency and intensity of the cross-border fighting, many of the lesser landowners erected smaller versions of these, often little more than a single tower. They were called pele, or peel, towers and Turton Tower, between Blackburn and Bolton, was one of the most southerly of these.

THE WALK

❶ With your back to the reservoir, take the grassy uphill path that leads off from the left-hand corner of the car park and bear right up steps to a stile. Climb it, walk across the moorland and climb another stile onto a tarmac track. Go through the kissing gate opposite, keep ahead, climb a stile onto a road and turn right.

❷ At a public footpath sign, turn sharp left along the track to Clough House Farm. At a junction of tracks just after passing through a gate, turn left along a wooded track, above a stream on the right. Cross a battlemented railway bridge and continue past Turton Tower to a road.

Turton Tower was originally a small and rather cramped medieval pele tower, subsequently extended and modernised to transform it into a comfortable residence. A pele tower was a defensive structure – basically a mini-castle – built mostly in the border counties of Cumbria, Durham and Northumberland as a protection against Scottish raids. It is rare to find one as far south as Lancashire, though Turton was probably built more for protection against feuding local families than against occasional Scottish raiders. In particular, the Orrells, who inherited the manor of Turton through marriage in the 15th century, needed the tower as a defence against some of their relatives, the De Lathom and Torboc families, who laid claims to the estate.

The original stone pele tower was built in the 15th century and, in the 16th century, the Orrells added several timber-framed structures. The cost of these additions led to financial problems and caused the family to sell the house in 1628 to Humphrey Chetham, a wealthy Manchester businessman and founder of the school and hospital in that city that bears his name.

There were several more changes of ownership before the house came into the possession of James Kay, another wealthy local businessman, in 1835. The Kays carried out a thorough restoration and reconstructed the north-east wing, adding the distinctive Dutch façade. After a succession of more owners, the house was taken over by Lancashire County Council in 1987 and is maintained as a museum.

It was James Kay who was mostly responsible for the present appearance of the house. He panelled many of the rooms, using in some instances 17th-century panelling salvaged from nearby demolished houses, and gave the building the sort of romantic Gothic appearance so popular with the Victorians. The house contains fine antique furniture and paintings in its recreated period rooms and is situated amidst attractive gardens and woodland.

For details of opening times and admission charges, telephone 01204 852203.

James Kay's son was responsible for the battlemented railway bridge, designed in this way in order to harmonise with the Gothic appearance of the tower. He also helped to finance the construction of the railway between Blackburn and Bolton, which was opened in 1845.

Turn left and at a public footpath sign, turn right over a stile and walk across a low brow, descending to a stile on the edge of woodland. Climb it, continue through the trees, descend steps and cross a bridge over Jumbles Reservoir.

❸   Turn left onto a path that keeps below a wooded embankment, first beside the reservoir and later beside a stream, to eventually reach a T-junction. Turn left to cross the stream, walk along a cobbled track and at a footpath post, turn right onto a path and recross the stream. At the next T-junction, turn left along another cobbled track to a road. Turn right uphill through Edgworth and, where the road curves right, turn left beside the Black Bull. Keep ahead along a path to the dam over Wayoh Reservoir and turn left to cross the dam.

> ### REFRESHMENTS
>
> There is a tearoom at Turton Tower and pubs at Edgworth. Near Entwistle station you pass the Strawbury Duck, a popular walkers' pub, with grand views over the surrounding moors. Although it looks older, it was built around 1900 but later extended into an adjacent cottage over 300 years old. There are small rooms and lots of nooks and crannies, the food is excellent and there is a varied and extensive menu (telephone: 01204 852013).

The adjacent Wayoh and Entwistle reservoirs are among several constructed in the valley of Bradshaw Brook in the 19th century. Entwistle is the oldest, built in 1832; Wayoh dates from 1876.

❹ On the other side, turn right onto a track beside the reservoir. At a fork, take the right-hand path to cross a causeway over an arm of the reservoir.

The impressive nine-arched Armsgrove Viaduct seen to the left was built in 1847-48 to take the Blackburn to Bolton railway across Bradshaw Brook.

On the other side, keep ahead along a tree-lined path, which winds uphill to a stile. Climb it, walk along the right edge of a field and, at a public footpath sign, turn right over a stile. Walk along an enclosed path, climb a stone stile and the path bends left to emerge onto a road. Keep ahead and follow the road to the left over a railway bridge to Entwistle station.

❺ Turn left at a public footpath sign to pass in front of the Strawbury Duck and continue along a track which descends, becomes tarmac, and crosses the dam of Entwistle Reservoir. Go through a gate at the far side of the dam, continue along a winding path beside the reservoir, turn left up steps and walk through trees to return to the start.

WALK 5

WHALLEY ABBEY AND THE DISSOLUTION OF THE MONASTERIES

Length: 5½ miles

The ruins of Whalley Abbey.

HOW TO GET THERE: Spring Wood Picnic Site is at the junction of the A671 and B6246, about ½ mile to the east of Whalley.

PARKING: At Spring Wood Picnic Site.

MAP: OS Explorer 287 (West Pennine Moors) GR 741360.

INTRODUCTION

The route of this exhilarating walk climbs over Whalley Nab, the prominent hill that rises above the Calder valley. Both the ascent and descent are quite steep but the stunning views across the Calder and Ribble valleys more than compensate for the effort. Near the end you walk beside the arches of an impressive Victorian railway viaduct and pass the interesting collection of ecclesiastical monuments in Whalley: monastic gatehouses, abbey ruins, a medieval church and Dark Age crosses.

HISTORICAL BACKGROUND

There were a number of reasons for Henry VIII's decision to close down the monasteries in the 1530s. After making the English church independent of the Pope and declaring himself Supreme Head of the Church in the 1530s, there was always the likelihood of a Roman Catholic backlash and the monasteries, with close links with their brethren on the continent, were an obvious source of danger. Additionally, the monasteries had become somewhat lax in their standards. But the major motive was greed: Henry wanted their money.

The king's minister, Thomas Cromwell, sent out a commission to enquire into the state of the monasteries in 1535. The subsequent report, as expected, painted a gloomy picture. On the basis of this Henry proceeded to carry out a wholesale

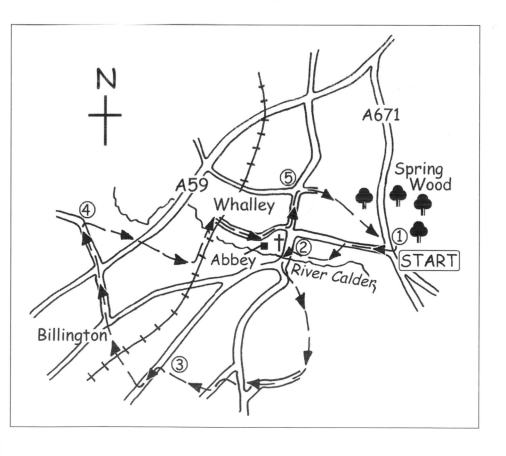

dissolution, in two stages: most of the smaller abbeys were dissolved in 1536 and the remaining ones in 1539. Perhaps this was a way of testing the waters, to see what the public reaction was to the closure of the smaller monasteries before continuing with the larger ones. As one of the smaller abbeys – there were probably fewer than 20 monks in residence at the time – Whalley was dissolved in the first wave.

In effect, such a momentous upheaval – the biggest change of land ownership in England since the Norman Conquest – caused surprisingly little reaction, except in the North where in 1536 it triggered a short-lived rebellion known as the Pilgrimage of Grace.

The vast monastic estates were acquired by the king and sold off to swell the royal coffers. Five of the abbey churches became cathedrals for new dioceses created by Henry – he originally intended to create more but greed got the better of him – and some were purchased by the local people for use as parish churches. But most, including Whalley Abbey, were either demolished, along with their attendant buildings, fell into ruin through neglect, or were used as a cheap source of building material by the local people.

THE WALK

Spring Wood was originally called Oxheywoode and was part of a deer park that belonged to the Abbot of Whalley. Following the dissolution of the monasteries it was sold, like most of the rest of the monastic estate, to the Assheton family. After several changes of ownership, it was bought by Lancashire County Council in the 1970s and developed into a picnic site and recreation area.

❶ Leave the car park, cross the A671 and walk down the road opposite, signposted to Whalley. At a public footpath sign, turn left over a stone stile, walk along an enclosed path, climb a stile, cross a track and climb another stile. Continue along a path which bends to the right beside the River Calder. Cross a footbridge and keep along a track by cottages to emerge onto the main road in Whalley.

❷ Turn left over Whalley Bridge, immediately turn left again to head steeply up Moor Lane and, at a public bridleway sign, bear left to continue uphill along an enclosed track through trees to a fork.

From here there are superb views over Whalley and the Calder valley.

At the fork, take the left-hand path rather than the right-hand bridleway – the views are better – continue uphill and the path bends right to rejoin the bridleway. Continue up over Whalley Nab to eventually emerge onto a tarmac track. Keep along it, go through a gate, walk along an enclosed tree-lined track

King Henry VIII.

and, on reaching a narrow lane, continue between farm buildings and cottages to a public footpath sign to Great Harwood. Do not keep ahead in the direction of the footpath sign but follow the lane around a right bend and continue steeply uphill over the Nab along this winding lane.

At a left bend, keep ahead along a track, turn left over a stile and walk across a field, bearing right away from its left-hand edge and making for a stone stile by a public footpath sign. Climb the stile, cross a lane, climb a stone stile opposite, walk along a right field edge and climb another stile in the corner onto a lane. Turn left, walk past farm buildings and at a public footpath sign, turn right over a stile. Bear left across a field, making for the left-hand edge of the trees ahead, where you climb a stile.

Now comes a magnificent view over the Ribble valley, which stays with you for much of the descent.

Head steeply downhill, keeping to the left of houses, cross a drive by a wall corner and continue down by the right field edge to climb a stile onto a road.

❸   Turn left, ignore the first public footpath sign on the right but at the second one, bear right down a track. The track – it soon becomes a tarmac one – bends right, passes between houses and continues down, over a railway bridge and along the left-hand edge of garden fences, to reach a road in Billington. Turn left. Take the first turning on the right, Elker Lane, and cross a bridge over the A59.

❹   Where the road bends left, turn right over a stile and walk along a field path, by a wire fence on the left. Climb a stile and continue straight across the next two fields. Climb a stile in the corner of the last field and follow the path to the right to cross, carefully, the busy A59. On the other side, turn left alongside a fence and turn right over a stile in that fence. Walk along the right field edge. Climb a stile, bear left along the left-hand edge of the next field and climb a kissing gate onto a road. Turn left and where the road ends, go through another kissing gate. Keep ahead along a track. Turn right towards the viaduct. Do not pass under it but turn left along an enclosed tarmac path beside it.

The Victorian brick-built railway viaduct carries the Blackburn-Clitheroe line across the Calder valley. It was constructed around the middle of the 19th century and has 49 arches. Note the pointed arches either side of the road that goes under it, built in the Gothic style to harmonise with the abbey.

Cross a footbridge over the River Calder. Keep ahead to a road and turn right to pass under the viaduct. Follow this road to the main street in Whalley, passing, in turn, the collection of buildings and monuments that make up Whalley's rich ecclesiastical heritage.

Whalley Abbey's most impressive buildings are the two gateways. First you pass under the north-west gateway, a fine vaulted structure built in the early 14th century. About 300 yards further on, you turn through the north-east gateway, the main entrance to the abbey ruins, erected in 1480.

The original abbey was at Stanlaw on the River Mersey, on a site now occupied by chemical works and oil refineries. Frequent flooding caused the Cistercian monks to seek a new location and the powerful Henry de Lacy, owner of Clitheroe Castle, granted them the site at Whalley beside the River Calder. The abbey was established here in 1296 and most of the buildings date from the 14th century.

Of the church, nothing is left apart from the foundations but there are substantial remains of some of the domestic buildings grouped around the cloister. The most complete survival is the cellarium, used by the lay brothers (these were people who worked and lived in the abbey but were not monks), which occupies the west side of the cloisters. Detached from the rest of the ruins and formerly used by the Roman Catholic Church, its future is currently the subject of debate.

The history of Whalley Abbey was fairly uneventful until its closure in 1536. As one of the smaller monasteries, Whalley was dissolved in 1536 but the last abbot, Richard Paslew, became involved, somewhat reluctantly, in the Pilgrimage of Grace. This was a rebellion against the dissolution of the monasteries and other recent religious changes that swept across much of northern England. The rebellion was quickly suppressed and Paslew was put on trial for treason. Not surprisingly he was found guilty and hanged at Lancaster in 1537.

REFRESHMENTS

There are four pubs in the centre of Whalley, all within a few yards of each other, plus several cafés and the Cloisters Coffee Shop at Whalley Abbey. The Dog Inn serves a wide variety of reasonably priced meals – sandwiches, jacket potatoes, salads, full cooked lunches – every day between 12 noon and 2 pm (telephone: 01254 823009).

Like most of the monasteries, Whalley and its estates passed into private hands and the monastic site became owned by the Assheton family of nearby Downham. A large house was built on the site of the former abbot's house and part of the infirmary. In 1923 this house and the remainder of the abbey buildings were purchased by the diocese of Manchester, thereby once more coming under church ownership. A few years later, the site passed to the new diocese of Blackburn and the house is now used as a conference and study centre. For details of opening times and admission charges, telephone 01254 828400.

Just beyond the abbey ruins is the parish church, much older than the abbey. There has been a place of worship on this site since Anglo-Saxon times but the present church dates mainly from the 13th century. The superb 15th-century choir stalls were salvaged from the abbey following the dissolution. Particularly interesting and rare are the three carved crosses in the churchyard. They date from somewhere between the 9th and 11th centuries and are thought to be Anglo-Celtic, with perhaps some Scandinavian influence.

Turn left along the main street through the village.

❺ Opposite Station Road, turn right along Brookes Lane. At a fork by a footpath post, take the right-hand track, go through a gate and continue along a track. Bear right to a stile in front of a gate, climb it and follow a worn grassy path, gently uphill across a field, bearing right away from its left-hand edge. Climb a stile on the far side. Follow a path through a narrow belt of trees to the A671 and cross over to return to the start.

Walk 6
Stonyhurst and Catholic Persecution

Length: 7½ miles

Stonyhurst College.

HOW TO GET THERE: The walk begins at the war memorial at Hurst Green, in the village centre, on the B6243 between Clitheroe and Longridge.

PARKING: Roadside parking at Hurst Green.

MAP: OS Explorer 287 (West Pennine Moors) GR 685379.

Introduction

This outstanding walk, full of historic interest and superb scenery, starts in the attractive village of Hurst Green and takes you past Stonyhurst, a great house that has had a most varied history and is now a prominent Catholic school. It includes magnificent views over the Ribble valley, some fine woodland and beautiful riverside walking beside the Hodder and Ribble. Part of the walk is along the Ribble Way and much of it follows a Tolkien Trail; the writer had strong links with this area.

HISTORICAL BACKGROUND

The creation of the Protestant Church of England by Elizabeth I, in 1559, made life difficult for the English Catholics. England's main enemies were the powerful continental Catholic countries – Spain and France – and therefore Catholics were considered to be potential traitors and enemy agents, rather like Communists were during the Cold War in the 20th century. This became particularly true after the Pope excommunicated Elizabeth in 1570, thus releasing her Catholic subjects from allegiance to her

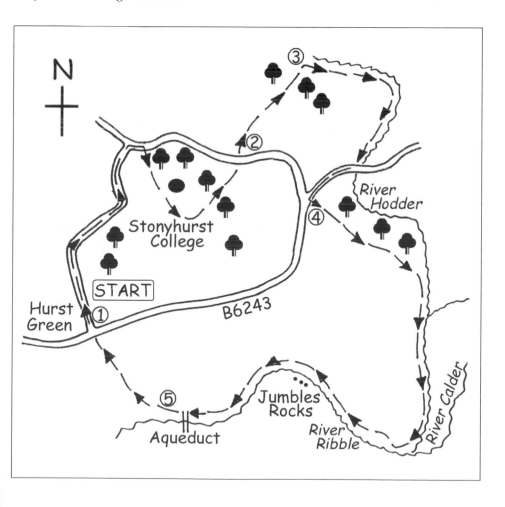

In the early years of Elizabeth's reign, persecution was fairly mild, comprising mostly fines for not attending Church of England services. It was after 1570 that persecution of the Catholics became more intense, not only because of the Pope's excommunication of Elizabeth but also because of the presence of Mary Queen of Scots on English soil. As a cousin of Elizabeth and a Roman Catholic, she was an obvious threat and over the following years became the focal point for a series of plots against the Queen. In the eyes of the Pope and the Catholic Church, Elizabeth was an illegitimate usurper and Mary the rightful queen of England as well as Scotland and the means by which England could be brought back into the Catholic fold.

As plots against Elizabeth increased and as more Catholic priests were smuggled into the country from the continent, persecution intensified. Fines for non-attendance at Anglican worship were considerably increased and both Catholic priests and those that sheltered them were regarded as felons and liable to be executed on suspicion of treason. That is why many Catholic houses throughout England had 'priest's holes' in which smuggled priests could be hidden from the authorities.

After a particularly serious plot in 1586, the Babington Plot in which Mary was directly implicated, Elizabeth reluctantly agreed to approve Mary's execution, which was carried out at Fotheringhay Castle in Northamptonshire in 1588. For the Pope and the continental Catholic powers, especially Spain, the only way now to restore Catholicism in England was invasion, hence the Spanish Armada. This polarised religion in England even more. Protestantism was identified with patriotism and a growing national pride whereas Roman Catholicism was un-English and synonymous with treachery.

During the Reformation, the North-West remained more Catholic than any other area of the country. This was because it was less susceptible to new ideas and influences from Europe than the South-East and, through the absence of large and prosperous towns, it was more reliant on the social amenities previously supplied by the monasteries. It is significant that the Pilgrimage of Grace, the only major revolt against the destruction of the monasteries by Henry VIII in the 1530s, was based in the North. Most of the great families in the area stayed loyal to the old religion and therefore suffered, at the best, suspicion and at the worst persecution, although most lived in harmony with their Protestant neighbours.

The death of Elizabeth and the removal – for the time being – of the Spanish threat did not end the persecution. Indeed, in the reigns of the first two Stuarts, James I and Charles I, matters worsened. The attempt by a group of Catholic conspirators to blow up king and Parliament in 1605 identified Catholics even more as potential traitors and the growth of a more extreme and therefore anti-Catholic Protestant movement, Puritanism, only increased suspicion and made persecution more intense.

THE WALK

❶ With your back to the Shireburn Arms, walk along Avenue Road, passing the Bayley Arms and some 18th-century almshouses. Keep ahead to enter the grounds of Stonyhurst College and, after a right bend, there is a glorious view ahead of the college buildings. On reaching the twin pools, follow the road to the left – the drive ahead is private – and the road bends right to a T-junction. Turn right and, where the road bends left, keep ahead, at a public footpath sign, along a tarmac track which passes in front of the college buildings.

Stonyhurst has certainly had a varied and chequered history. The imposing Elizabethan mansion was begun by Sir Richard Shireburn in 1592 and completed in the early 17th century. The gardens were laid out later in that century. Although Sir Richard embraced the new Protestant religion – somewhat half-heartedly and purely for political expediency – other members of the Shireburn family remained loyal to the Catholic faith and therefore inevitably attracted suspicion. During the Civil War, the Shireburns, along with most Catholic landowners, were Royalists but in 1648 they were forced to give hospitality to Oliver Cromwell at the time of the Battle of Preston. As a Parliamentary commander and aggressive Puritan he was not exactly a welcome guest in a Catholic household.

The Shireburn male line died out and in the 18th century the house passed by marriage to the Welds, a Catholic family from Dorset. They abandoned Stonyhurst in favour of their main residence, Lulworth Castle, and the house became derelict.

Around the time that Stonyhurst was built, an English Catholic college, staffed by Jesuits, had been set up on the continent, initially in France and later in Flanders. During the intense anti-Catholic fervour that accompanied the French Revolution in the 1790s, the Jesuits were expelled and homeless and in 1794 Thomas Weld offered them the neglected and by now semi-derelict Stonyhurst. The offer was accepted gladly. The original buildings were restored and considerably extended and in the 1830s St Peter's church was built, based on the design of King's College Chapel at Cambridge. The wheel had turned full circle: a former Catholic house was rescued from oblivion and dereliction to become one of the foremost Catholic schools in England.

The tour of the house, although inevitably restricted, takes in both the later extensions, built since the college was established, and the original Elizabethan mansion and includes the Great Hall, in which you see the table on which Cromwell is reputed to

Oliver Cromwell.

have slept in 1648. It also takes in the church and there is a museum. From the gardens there are fine views over the Ribble valley.

The Tolkien connection comes from the fact that J.R.R. Tolkien and members of his family regularly stayed at Stonyhurst. One of his sons, John, who was studying for the priesthood in Rome, was evacuated here during the Second World War and Michael, another son, taught at the college in the late 1960s and early 1970s. Tolkien spent a lot of his time writing while here, including working on Lord of the Rings, *and it is thought that the local countryside provided the inspiration for some of the scenes in his books.*

Stonyhurst College is generally open for six weeks from the middle of July until the end of August. For details, telephone 01254 826345.

Keep along the track which curves left and continues between hedges. Where it bends right, turn left, initially onto a narrow path alongside farm buildings on the right and later along a tarmac track to reach a road.

There are outstanding views from here of the Ribble valley, Pendle Hill and Clitheroe Castle.

❷ Cross over and take the track opposite, which becomes fence-lined. Where the track curves left, keep ahead to climb a ladder stile and continue along the right edge of Over Hacking Wood. Look out for where a stile on the left admits you to the wood. Walk at first along its right inside edge and then descend a long flight of steps through the densely packed trees to cross a footbridge over a stream.

❸ Keep ahead, turn right over another footbridge and head uphill to emerge in front of Hodder Place. Now continue downhill and after going through a kissing gate, keep ahead along an enclosed track beside the tree-lined River Hodder. The track follows the river around a right-hand bend – going through a series of kissing gates – to emerge onto a road at Lower Hodder Bridge.

Ahead is a picturesque old packhorse bridge over the Hodder called Cromwell's Bridge, built in the 16th century by Sir Richard Shireburn. It is so-called because Cromwell is alleged to have crossed it on his way to the Battle of Preston in 1648, but it is now considered more likely that he crossed the river elsewhere.

Turn right uphill, now joining the Ribble Way for the remainder of the walk.

❹ Just beyond a road junction on the right, turn left over a ladder stile. Walk across a field and, after climbing a stile, keep by the left-hand edge of a field to climb another stile. Continue over a brow along the left-hand edge of the next field but before reaching the corner, the path bears right to a kissing gate. Go through, veer slightly left across a field and on the far side, go through a kissing gate onto a tarmac track. Turn left downhill – Winckley Hall is to the right – and keep ahead through a farmyard. Follow the main track, first to the right and then to the left, and turn right again along an enclosed track beside the Hodder to reach the confluence of the Hodder and Ribble.

REFRESHMENTS

There are three pubs at Hurst Green. The Eagle and Child does an excellent range of meals – from sandwiches to full Sunday lunches – at very reasonable prices (telephone: 01254 826207). A tearoom at Stonyhurst College is open to the public from approximately mid-July to the end of August (telephone: 01254 826345).

The route continues along the left-hand edge of riverside meadows and later an enclosed track to the confluence of the Ribble and Calder. On the opposite side of the Ribble is Hacking Hall. Continue by the Ribble – a beautiful stretch – and where the path narrows just before reaching a stone building, turn right up steps and climb a ladder stile onto a track. Turn left, passing Jumbles Rocks. Turn left in front of Jumbles Farm and where the tarmac track curves right, keep ahead along the left edge of riverside meadows again. Continue over a succession of stiles by the river, following it around a right-hand curve to reach an aqueduct.

The aqueduct was constructed in the 1880s to carry water from Whitewell to Blackburn.

Climb a stile to the right of the aqueduct, keep ahead and climb another stile on the edge of woodland.

❺ Immediately cross a footbridge over a stream and climb steps through the trees, curving right and then bending left to a stile. Turn right over it and keep ahead by woodland on the right. Re-enter the trees, cross two plank footbridges and climb another stile. Follow the path gently uphill along a low narrow ridge between streams on both sides and look out for a waymarked post which directs you to cross the stream on the right. Continue uphill by the left-hand field edge and climb a stone stile in the top corner. Walk through the car park of the Shireburn Arms to return to the start.

WALK 7

HOGHTON TOWER AND THE UNION OF THE ENGLISH AND SCOTTISH CROWNS

Length: 3½ miles

Hoghton Tower occupies a commanding hilltop position.

HOW TO GET THERE: Hoghton is on the A675 between Blackburn and Preston. The walk begins in front of the Boars Head.	**PARKING:** Use the nearby side roads rather than the busy main road.	**MAP:** OS Explorer 287 (West Pennine Moors) GR 614266.

INTRODUCTION

Hoghton Tower, visited by James I in 1617, stands on a wooded hill and this pleasant walk provides both fine views of the house and extensive vistas over the surrounding countryside. The middle section is most dramatic as you walk through the narrow, wooded Hoghton gorge, below the eastern slopes of the hill and beside the cascading River Darwen.

HISTORICAL BACKGROUND

The origins of the eventual union of the crowns of England and Scotland go back to the beginning of the 16th century. Henry VII was anxious to secure his northern frontier by making peace with Scotland and in 1502 he negotiated a marriage between his daughter Margaret and James IV of Scotland. The arrangement worked and peace was maintained for the duration of Henry's reign but hostilities were rekindled under his son, Henry VIII. In 1513 James IV was killed during the heavy defeat suffered by the Scottish army at the Battle of Flodden.

He was succeeded first by James V and then by Mary Queen of Scots but in 1567 Mary, a Catholic queen in a predominantly Protestant country, was forced to flee from Scotland. She crossed the border into England and threw herself on the mercy of her cousin, Elizabeth I. Mary's presence in England was a severe embarrassment and potentially a source of great danger to Elizabeth. During her nineteen years of imprisonment in England in a variety of castles, Mary was frequently the focal point of Catholic plots to topple Elizabeth and replace her as queen. In the eyes of the Pope and Catholic Church, Elizabeth I was illegitimate and a heretic, and Mary was the rightful queen of England. Finally Elizabeth, on

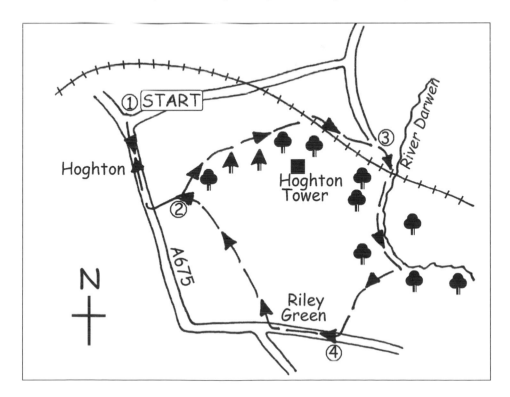

the advice of her ministers, reluctantly agreed to Mary's execution. This was carried out at Fotheringhay Castle in Northamptonshire in 1587.

Ironically, the heir to the childless, unmarried and increasingly aged Elizabeth was Mary's son, James VI of Scotland. Unlike his mother he was a Protestant and he was acceptable to the English Parliament as heir to the throne. Accordingly, on the death of Elizabeth in 1603, James journeyed southwards to claim his new kingdom and was crowned James I in Westminster Abbey. For the first time in their often violent history, the kingdoms of England and Scotland now shared the same monarch and this was to pave the way for the eventual union of the two countries just over a century later.

James I made a number of journeys around England and in 1617 he paid a memorable visit to Hoghton Tower.

THE WALK

❶ Start by the Boars Head and, with your back to the pub, turn left along the road. Opposite the war memorial, turn left along the drive towards Hoghton Tower. Where the drive starts to rise by a lodge, the route continues to the left along a track. At this point you keep straight ahead along the drive to visit the house.

James I's connection with Hoghton Tower came on a visit that the king made there in 1617. Allegedly, he was so delighted with the hospitality he received that he knighted a loin of beef. It is likely that he did this in jest as, contrary to popular myth, this event is not the origin of the word 'sirloin'; this comes from the French surlonge. Incidentally,

The gatehouse at Hoghton Tower.

the cost of entertaining the king and his huge retinue almost bankrupted the host, Sir Richard de Hoghton, who was forced to spend some time in a debtor's prison shortly afterwards.

Hoghton Tower occupies a commanding hilltop position between Blackburn and Preston and, despite having a decidedly medieval and fortress-like appearance, it is an Elizabethan house, built in 1565 by Sir Thomas de Hoghton. Like many of the Lancashire nobility, Sir Thomas remained true to the Catholic faith during the troubled years of the Reformation and died as an exile in the Netherlands. Later members of the family, however, accepted the reformed Protestant church and thus escaped the anti-Catholic persecution of the 17th century.

The buildings, which are entered through a battlemented gatehouse,

King James I in hunting dress.

are grouped around two courtyards and the state rooms occupy the inner courtyard. Most of these rooms, which include the king's bedchamber (where James slept), state bedchamber and banqueting room, possess fine furniture and panelling and of particular interest is the impressive banqueting hall, which has a minstrels' gallery and contains the table at which James I is supposed to have knighted the loin of beef. Other features of interest in the house are the Tudor well house, dungeons, underground passages and a collection of dolls and dolls houses. In addition, there are attractive grounds and walled gardens, from which there are superb and extensive views over the surrounding countryside.

During the 18th century, the house was abandoned and fell into disrepair. The family returned during the Victorian period and, in the 1870s, Sir Henry de Hoghton began an extensive programme of restoration, which has been continued by subsequent owners.

Hoghton Tower is usually open during July, August and September and on bank holidays. For details of opening times and admission charges, telephone 01254 852986.

❷   After turning left – a right turn if retracing your steps from the house – walk along the track to where it ends and climb a stile. Keep ahead along the right-hand edge of a field, by a wall on the right, and after climbing two more stiles you enter woodland. Head downhill through the trees, later bearing left away from the wall and continuing down to a railway line. Cross it carefully and turn right along a track. Descend to a T-junction in the hamlet of Hoghton Bottoms and turn right along a track.

> **REFRESHMENTS**
>
> There are two pubs at Hoghton and refreshments can also be obtained at Hoghton Tower (open bank holidays and July to September). The route passes the Royal Oak at Riley Green, a cosy and welcoming country pub, with log fires in winter and a wide range of bar and restaurant meals (telephone: 01254 201445).

❸   Where the track bends left, keep ahead along a path beside the river through the beautiful, wooded and narrow Hoghton gorge, passing under a railway viaduct.

The water power provided by the River Darwen led to the establishment of mills here and elsewhere along the valley bottom. The five-arched railway viaduct, an outstanding example of Victorian engineering, carries the East Lancashire line between Blackburn and Preston across the Hoghton gorge. The line was opened in 1846.

After climbing a ladder stile, veer slightly right away from the river to join a track, which bends right and heads uphill to a kissing gate. Go through and at a fork, take the left-hand track and follow it to a road.

❹   Turn right into Riley Green and turn right again along a tarmac track beside the Royal Oak. Where the track ends, climb a ladder stile and head gently uphill across a field.

As you walk uphill, there is a fine view of Hoghton Tower to the right.

After climbing a stile at the top, keep ahead along a track through trees to another stile. Climb that and head downhill by the right-hand field edge. At the bottom, go through a kissing gate onto the tarmac drive leading to the house. Turn left, here picking up the outward route, and retrace your steps to the start.

WALK 8

PENDLE HILL AND 17TH-CENTURY WITCHCRAFT

Length: 6 miles

The mysterious and brooding Pendle Hill.

HOW TO GET THERE: Barley lies on a minor road between Downham and the A6068 at Fence. The walk begins from the car park and picnic site.

PARKING: In the pay-and-display car park at Barley.

MAP: OS Explorer OL 41 (Forest of Bowland & Ribblesdale) GR 823403.

INTRODUCTION

You do not climb Pendle Hill on this walk – that delight can be left to another day – but the hill is there in the background throughout, brooding over the landscape, and there is a series of magnificent views of it from different angles. The route explores the attractive countryside at its base, a mixture of fields, streams, woodland, moorland, old farmhouses and new reservoirs, and passes through two villages that have strong links with the story of the Pendle Witches.

HISTORICAL BACKGROUND

During the Middle Ages and on into the 16th and 17th centuries, times of ignorance and superstition, allegations of witchcraft flourished and it was easy for anyone who was a bit different or had strange habits to be accused of being a witch. This was especially true of simple old women who perhaps dressed in black, muttered to themselves, kept a black cat, or were able to cure people of various ailments by using herbs and other natural remedies. At the time, many people regarded witches as evil and believed that they were in league with the Devil.

Persecution became much harsher after the accession of James I in 1603. The king had something of an obsession with witchcraft and had written a book, *Daemonology*, about witches and their practices. His coming to the throne led to an increase in anti-witch hysteria and in 1604 an act was passed which made it a capital offence to 'consult, covenant with, entertain, employ, feed, or reward any evil and wicked spirit, or to utter spells'.

The most famous incident concerning witches occurred in the spring of 1612 and involved a number of women from the Pendle Hill area. Two old women from rival peasant families, Annie Whittle and Elizabeth Southerns – nicknamed

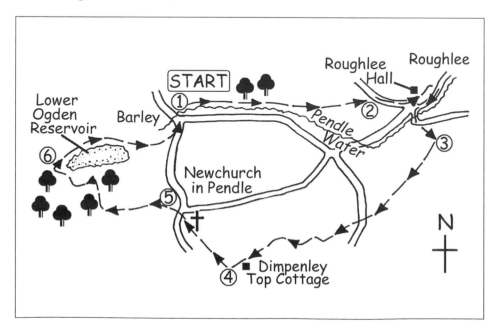

Chattox and Old Demdike respectively – were widely thought to have special powers. A feud seems to have developed between the two families and during the course of investigations carried out by a local magistrate, several people made allegations of witchcraft against both women and others in the locality, accusing them of putting curses on people to cause illness, madness or even death, causing animals to go lame and – most unforgivable – turning the ale sour in a local inn.

After interrogation, the women confessed to their alleged crimes, not surprising since they were mostly simple and ignorant old women, and they were sent for trial at Lancaster Castle. Following a meeting between several more families held on Good Friday at Malkin Tower, the home of Old Demdike – the site of which is unknown – more suspected witches were sent to Lancaster. Among these was Alice Nutter, a reasonably well-educated woman from the village of Roughlee.

The trial took place on 17th August 1612. The verdict was a foregone conclusion as none of the accused was provided with a defence lawyer. On 20th August nine of them were hanged outside the castle walls, though Old Demdike escaped the hangman's noose: she died in prison just before the start of the trial.

Thomas Potts, clerk to the judge, publicised the trial by publishing a book in the following year called *The Wonderful Discovery of Witches in the County of Lancaster*. Over the following centuries, stories of the Pendle Witches were spread throughout the country, boosted by novels such as Harrison Ainsworth's *The Lancashire Witches* (1848) and Robert Neill's *Mist Over Pendle* (1951). In recent years, the story of the Pendle Witches has helped to promote tourism in this part of Lancashire.

THE WALK

❶ Begin by taking the path that leads off from the far end of the car park through trees. Continue along a track beside Pendle Water on the right, passing by a former mill and between cottages, to where the track turns right over a bridge. Go through a gate and keep ahead along a path, still beside Pendle Water. Shortly after climbing a stile, bear left away from the stream and climb steeply through woodland to a stile. Climb it and bear right across a field, looking out for a waymarked stile in a fence. After climbing it, the route continues in a straight line across a series of fields and through a succession of stiles and gates. Finally, you climb a stile in the right-hand corner of the last field onto a lane.

❷ Turn right downhill into Roughlee. Just before reaching a road, turn left along a track, passing houses and continuing in front of Roughlee Hall.

Roughlee Hall, a handsome 17th-century building, was the alleged home of Alice Nutter. She was the odd one out of the Pendle Witches. All the others were simple, poor and uneducated women while Alice came from a reasonably well-off background and it has always been something of a mystery as to how and why she became associated with Chattox, Old Demdike and the others. The hall is now split into private homes and is not open to the public.

At a T-junction, turn right to the road and turn right again through the village.

Opposite the Bay Horse Inn, turn left over a bridge. Head uphill and, at a sharp left bend, keep ahead up a paved path. Almost immediately bear left off it and continue across grass and over a track to a stile. Climb it, keep ahead uphill by a wall on the left and climb another stile.

❸ Turn right onto a tarmac track alongside a reservoir wall.

All the way along this ridge top path, there are magnificent views of Pendle Hill over to the right.

At a fork, take the right-hand enclosed track and, where the track ends, climb a stone stile. Walk along the left edge of a field and climb two stiles in quick succession onto a road. Keep ahead and, at a public footpath sign, turn right over a stile. Bear left diagonally across a field and cross a tarmac track to reach the corner of a wall.

Continue across the next field, looking for a stile about 50 yards to the right of the field corner. After climbing it, continue along a tarmac track, which bends right downhill and then bends left. In front of a house, bear left along a track which curves right and continues downhill to Lower Dimpenley Farm. Turn left along a track, by a stream on the right, passing Dimpenley Top Cottage on the left and a sewage works on the right.

❹ Immediately after passing a stile on the left, turn right onto a narrow enclosed path, between the sewage works fence on the right and a high hedge on the left. Go through a kissing gate and head steadily uphill along the left edge of a field towards the houses of Newchurch in Pendle. Pass through a gap in the field corner, continue up an enclosed path and turn left into the churchyard at Newchurch.

The 'new church' dates from 1544 and was mainly rebuilt in the 18th century. Look out for the 'Eye of God', a gap in the stonework at the base of the tower. It was believed that this was to watch over the local people and protect them from witchcraft. In the village, the Witches Galore shop sells all sorts of books and souvenirs of the Pendle Witches.

At the top end of the churchyard, go through a gate onto a road and turn right.

❺ Just before a road junction, turn left up steps, beside the public toilets. Go through a kissing gate and continue up more steps to a stile. Climb it and follow the direction of the yellow arrows uphill across rough grassland, making for a Pendle Way sign in the wall on the right.

From here enjoy more impressive views of Pendle, rising above the waters of the reservoirs.

Continue uphill beside the wall. Climb a stile and keep ahead, still by the wall. Just before reaching the field corner, turn right over a stile. Walk downhill along a path beside a conifer plantation on the left. Turn left over a stile and continue along a clear path through the plantation. The path curves right and descends a long flight of steps to emerge from the conifers. It later bends sharp right and continues down more steps to a footbridge. After crossing the bridge, follow a winding path which crosses another footbridge to reach a gate.

❻ Go through the gate and turn right along a track beside Lower Ogden Reservoir.

Irish navvies helped in the construction of both the Lower and Upper Ogden reservoirs, built to provide water to the Nelson area. Upper Ogden was completed in 1906 and Lower Ogden in 1914.

Follow this track – it later becomes tarmac – downhill back to Barley.

WALK 9

LANCASTER AND TRADE WITH THE AMERICAS

Length: 6½ miles

HOW TO GET THERE: Lancaster is situated on the A6, in the north-west of the county and the walk begins in the Market Square.

PARKING: There are a number of pay-and-display car parks in Lancaster.

MAP: OS Explorer 296 (Lancaster, Morecambe & Fleetwood) GR 476617.

INTRODUCTION

Lancaster is one of the finest Georgian towns in the country and there is plenty of opportunity to enjoy the exceptional quality of the architecture, as well as the medieval castle and priory, before descending past the remains of Roman baths to the River Lune, a bustling centre of commercial activity in the 18th century when Lancaster was an important port. After a pleasant walk beside the estuary and above marshland, the route heads inland across fields, to return along the towpath of the Lancaster Canal.

HISTORICAL BACKGROUND

Lancaster occupies a vital strategic position, lying on the west coast route between England and Scotland, between the Pennines and the sea, and at the lowest crossing point on the River Lune. Both Roman and Norman conquerors were aware of this: the Romans built a fort above the river and, around 1,000 years later, the Normans erected a castle on the same site.

Despite its military importance – and the fact that it was the county town of Lancashire – Lancaster remained a relatively small town until its heyday as a port. British trade with the trans-Atlantic colonies expanded rapidly from around 1720 onwards and many west coast towns experienced increased growth and prosperity as a result. The great ports of Liverpool and Bristol were the main beneficiaries but smaller ports, such as Lancaster and Whitehaven, were also well placed to reap some of the rewards.

Lancaster's 'golden age' was during the last 30 years of the 18th century when trade with the American and Caribbean colonies boomed, and the many fine Georgian buildings in the city are a reflection of Lancaster's prosperity at the time. It all began with the construction of St George's Quay in 1750 and the building of the Customs House in 1764. These provided the port with the most

The 18th-century Customs House at Lancaster is now the Maritime Museum.

up-to-date facilities and, over the following three decades, trade between America and the Lune estuary expanded rapidly.

Among the main commodities in this trade were sugar, coffee, rum, cotton, timber and slaves. Like the other west coast ports, Lancaster played a major role in the slave trade, perhaps surprisingly so in view of the large Quaker element

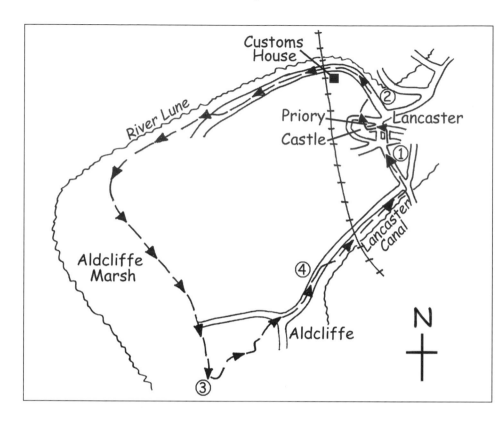

among its business community, but the anti-slavery movement in England had yet to begin.

The local Quakers were among the most enterprising and wealthy merchants and manufacturers and played a major role in the development of the port. One of them, Robert Lawson, had been responsible for the building of a quay further downstream at Sunderland Point in 1720. This was an attempt to overcome the problem of the silting up of the Lune, one of the difficulties that caused Lancaster's heyday to be relatively short-lived. Another attempt to build a port further down the river at Glasson Dock did little to halt the decline. The other major problem was the town's comparative distance and isolation from the main manufacturing centres in south Lancashire. Efforts were also made to overcome this difficulty by constructing first the Lancaster Canal, to provide a link with Preston and the growing cotton towns to the south, and later the railway. None of these measures were successful and during the 19th century Lancaster lost its commercial importance. Much of the legacy from that 'golden age' survives, however, in its superb streets, terraces, quayside and imposing public buildings.

THE WALK

Dominating the Market Square is one of Lancaster's handsome Georgian buildings, the Old Town Hall (now the City Museum), built in 1781-83. Many of the streets in the city centre are lined with elegant Georgian houses and an exploration of these is well worthwhile. Some of the finest are to be found in Church Street, around Castle Park and Castle Hill and the adjacent streets, and along St George's Quay. All of these streets feature in the first part of the walk.

Two individual buildings, passed between the Market Square and the castle, that deserve particular attention are the Music Room and Judge's Lodgings. The Music Room, one of Lancaster's smaller Georgian buildings, dates from around 1735 and was possibly a pavilion or summerhouse for one of the larger houses. The Judge's Lodgings is earlier, a grand and well-proportioned 17th-century town house, where the judges used to stay while presiding over cases at the castle. Now it houses a collection of dolls and impressive examples of furniture made by the well-known local Gillow firm. For details of opening times and admission charges to the Judge's Lodgings, telephone 01524 32808.

❶ Facing the Old Town Hall, pass to the left of it and turn right under an arch into Music Room Passage. Walk past the Music Room, continue along Sun Street and, at a crossroads, turn left along Church Street. In front of the Judge's Lodgings, take the cobbled uphill street to the left to the gatehouse of Lancaster Castle. Turn right, follow the castle walls round to the left and climb a flight of steps to the priory.

Lancaster Castle has been restored and extended several times throughout its history to enable it to retain two of its original functions, as a prison and as the county's law courts. Of the original Norman castle, built by Roger de Poitou around 1090, the much restored keep survives. The curtain walls, towers and the castle's most striking feature – John of Gaunt's great gatehouse – were constructed in the late 14th and 15th centuries. A major rebuilding and extension took place in the 18th century when the semi-circular Shire Hall was built.

Royal connections with the castle began when John of Gaunt, fourth son of Edward III, married Blanche of Lancaster. After deposing Richard II in 1399, their son ascended the throne as Henry IV, first of the Lancastrian kings. Since then all monarchs – female as well as male – have held the title Duke of Lancaster. Among many important trials and executions that have been held here are those of John Paslew, last abbot of Whalley in 1536, the Pendle Witches in 1612 and Jacobite prisoners after the rebellions of 1715 and 1745.

Because the castle is still used as a prison and court, visitors can only be taken on a restricted tour. This usually includes the Shire Hall, noted for its large collection of shields, Crown Court, dungeons and aptly-named Drop Room, through which condemned prisoners passed to their execution at Hanging Corner, often watched by large crowds. For details of opening times and admission charges, telephone 01524 64998.

The fine 15th-century church, which stands next to the castle, was originally part of a Benedictine priory, founded around 1094 by the same man who built the first castle. It was one of a number of alien priories in England, which means it was the dependency of a continental monastery, in this case, the abbey of Sees in Normandy. During the Hundred Years War with France, these alien priories were regarded almost as enemy spy bases and in 1414 they were suppressed by Henry V. Lancaster Priory was handed over to a nunnery in Middlesex and converted into a parish church. The impressive west tower was rebuilt in the 18th century.

Turn right along a tarmac path in front of the church, by a footpath sign to 'Roman Bath House, Maritime Museum and St George's Quay'. Head downhill and at the next Roman Bath House sign, turn right across grass for a brief detour to the remains of the bath house.

These sparse remains are the only piece of Roman Lancaster still visible on their original site. They are of a bath house that lay just outside the walls of the fort and were only discovered and excavated in the early 1970s.

Return to the main path, continue downhill – down steps in places – and finally turn right to emerge onto St George's Quay.

❷ Turn left beside the River Lune, passing old warehouses, to the Maritime Museum.

St George's Quay was built around the middle of the 18th century in order that the port could accommodate the growing trade with the American and Caribbean colonies. It is lined with original 18th-century warehouses and some 20th-century imitations, which blend in well with the originals. Many of these have been converted into stylish apartments.

Finest of all the buildings lining the quayside – and arguably the most handsome of all Lancaster's Georgian buildings – is the beautifully proportioned Customs House. This was built in 1764 to the design of George Gillow, a member of the well-known local furniture company. Nowadays, it serves a most appropriate function as a Maritime Museum, depicting the rise and fall of Lancaster as a port and also the maritime history of the whole Morecambe Bay area. For details of opening times and admission charges, telephone 01524 64637.

Continue past the museum, go under a railway bridge and keep ahead. At a public footpath sign to Aldcliffe Hall Lane, take the tarmac track ahead and then bear right to continue along an attractive grassy path beside the

> **REFRESHMENTS**
>
> You will find a wide choice of pubs, cafés and restaurants in the centre of Lancaster.

estuary. The path eventually reaches a fingerpost. Keep ahead to a stile, climb it and continue along the top of an embankment above Aldcliffe Marsh, following the curve of the estuary gradually to the left.

As well as fine views across the Lune estuary, the skyline of Lancaster can be seen over to the left.

At a public footpath sign, turn left over a stile and keep ahead. At a Lancashire Coastal Way sign, turn right through a gate and walk along a straight, enclosed track.

❸ At a public footpath sign to Aldcliffe Hall Lane, turn left to descend steps. Cross a footbridge and walk along the right-hand edge of a field. Climb a stile in the corner and turn left along the left-hand edge of the next two fields, but look out for where you turn left over a stile. Turn right and continue along an enclosed path, negotiating two stiles and two gates, to eventually emerge onto a lane. Turn right into Aldcliffe and turn left at a T-junction.

❹ On meeting the Lancaster Canal, keep ahead along its towpath into the town.

The Lancaster Canal was constructed in the 1790s to link the town with Preston and the main centres of industry and population to the south and with Kendal and the Lake District to the north. It was hoped that it would prolong Lancaster's prosperity but the rise of more favourably situated ports and the continued silting up of the River Lune put paid to that.

Just in front of a road bridge, climb a short flight of steps. Do not continue up the second flight to the bridge but turn left along Penny Street. Turn right into Market Street to return to the start.

WALK 10

WYCOLLER AND THE EARLY TEXTILE INDUSTRY

Length: 8 or 6 miles

The ancient packhorse bridge at Wycoller Hall.

HOW TO GET THERE: Haworth Road car park and picnic area in Wycoller Country Park lies on a minor road between Laneshawbridge and Haworth about 2½ miles south-east of Colne.

PARKING: Haworth Road car park.

MAP: OS Explorer OL 21 (South Pennines) GR 937394.

INTRODUCTION

This varied and highly scenic walk begins at Wycoller, now a peaceful country park with an atmospheric ruined hall, but once a thriving community that depended on handloom weaving. The walk continues through pastureland, wooded valleys and open moorland, with a visit to a waterfall and Trawden, an old mining and textile village. The full walk also includes an optional climb to the summit of Boulsworth Hill, from where there are magnificent views across the Brontë moors. The route is easy to follow as most of it uses well waymarked trails – the Pendle Way, Brontë Way and Brontës in Pendle Circular Walk – but there is some rough walking in places and a beck to ford. The latter could be difficult after heavy or prolonged rain.

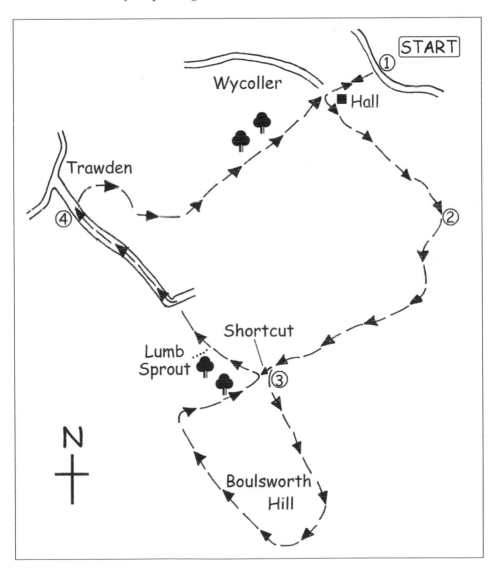

HISTORICAL BACKGROUND

When we think of the textile industry we tend to think of huge Victorian mills dominating the skyline of densely-packed large industrial towns, like those depicted in the paintings of L.S. Lowry. But before the Industrial Revolution – and even well on into it – the textile industry was a mainly small rural industry. It was also a cottage-based industry, with the work carried out by people in their own homes using simple hand-operated machines. Sometimes the work was combined with other activities, such as farming, and the spinning and weaving was done chiefly by the female or younger members of the family to supplement what the men earned on the land, hence the origin of the word 'spinster' for young unmarried women.

This was known as the domestic system. The whole process was organised by a merchant or manufacturer who employed people, generally called putters-out, to distribute the work to the people in their homes and to collect the finished work when completed.

In the 18th century, three inventions by local Lancastrians, mainly using water and later steam power, considerably speeded up the spinning process. In 1765 James Hargreaves invented the Spinning Jenny which could spin a number of threads at once. This was small enough to be housed in a cottage and was still operated by hand. More significant was Richard Arkwright's Water Frame, which was developed around 1769 and was powered by water. Samuel Crompton's Mule, which combined the best features of both the Jenny and Water Frame – hence its name – completed the trio of inventions in 1781. This produced both fine and strong yarn and could be adapted to the making of all kinds of textiles.

The invention of powered machines, first in the spinning and later in the weaving processes, signalled the end of the domestic system. Workers soon had to go to work in sheds, built to house this new machinery, i.e. factories. Ultimately all parts of the textile manufacturing process took place in factories and mainly in an urban setting, but this was a gradual rather than a sudden process as the advance of machinery and the growth of factories inevitably took a long time and varied from area to area.

In the remoter valleys and villages of the Pennines, such as Wycoller, handloom weaving continued well into the middle years of the 19th century but in the end, lacking both the sources of power and decent transport, they also declined and sank into decay and obscurity.

THE WALK

❶ With your back to the road, go down steps to the right of an information board and head down to a kissing gate.

Immediately there is a magnificent view across the valley to the right looking towards Colne, with its hilltop church and town hall clearly visible, backed by the unmistakeable profile of Pendle Hill. As you continue downhill, you see many examples of vaccary walls, upright slabs of stone that mark the field boundaries. It is thought that these were used to enclose cattle – vaccary comes from the French word vache (cow) – and date back to the Middle Ages.

Go through the kissing gate, continue downhill and descend steps to the ruins of Wycoller Hall.

Wycoller was originally a small agricultural settlement in the Forest of Trawden but, with sheep pastures on the surrounding moorland and a good supply of water, it later developed into a centre for handloom weaving. By 1820 the population of Wycoller had peaked at around 350. The introduction of the power loom ultimately spelt doom for the handloom weavers and Wycoller also suffered from a remote location. Its population dropped to 231 in 1851 and 107 by 1871. By the 1950s the village was almost deserted and the cottages abandoned and derelict. At several times there were threats to flood the valley to provide extra water supplies to Colne and the surrounding area.

In 1973 the village, valley and surrounding farms were taken over by Lancashire County Council who created a country park and conservation area. Since then visitors – especially walkers – have come into the area, the cottages have been restored, a craft centre and café have opened and the extensive network of public rights of way have been supplemented by the creation of new concessionary paths.

The village – in fact, little more than a hamlet – has some attractive old handloom weavers' cottages but the main building is the ruined but highly atmospheric Wycoller Hall. In the late 18th century, the original Tudor building was extended by its owner, the extravagant Henry Cunliffe, who bankrupted himself in the process. As a result, after his death in 1818, the estate was split up and the hall gradually fell into ruins. It was allegedly visited by the Brontë sisters and it is claimed to be the setting for Ferndean Manor in Charlotte Brontë's Jane Eyre. *Next to the hall is a fine 17th-century aisled barn, now a visitor centre.*

Wycoller is also noted for its varied array of bridges – seven in all – over the beck. Amongst the finest are the picturesque packhorse and clapper bridges near the hall, and the clam bridge a little further up the valley.

Turn right towards the packhorse bridge. Do not cross it but turn sharp left along a track. Follow it through the valley beside Wycoller Beck on the right, and at a fork by a fingerpost, take the right-hand upper track to Dean House Farm. Walk through the farmyard, go through a gate and keep ahead to climb a stile. Continue gently uphill and at the corner of the wall on the right, keep ahead up to a ladder stile. After climbing it, continue to a fingerpost in front of a wall.

❷ Turn right and follow a winding and undulating path across rough moorland to a gate. Go through and keep ahead to a fingerpost. Turn right to ford the beck

The spinning jenny.

and clamber up the steep bank on the other side. Turn left and the path – slabbed in places – continues across moorland at the base of Boulsworth Hill, by a wall on the right most of the time. Eventually descend to go through a kissing gate and join a tarmac track. Continue along it until you reach a ladder stile on the right.

❸ Turn right over it if doing the shorter route and continue at * below. For the full walk that takes you to the summit of Boulsworth Hill, keep ahead for about 50 yards and just in front of gateposts, turn left onto a concrete track, signposted 'Boulsworth Hill Circular Walk'. After passing to the left of a water treatment plant, the route continues more steeply uphill along a rough path – well marked with regular footpath posts – to a kissing gate. Go through and head up to the ridge where the path bends right and continues up to the pile of boulders and trig point that marks the summit.

At a height of 1,696 feet, the views from the summit of Boulsworth Hill are magnificent and extend from Pendle Hill across to the Brontë moors.

Past the trig point the path now curves right and heads downhill – quite steeply at times – to a stile. Climb it, keep ahead by a wall on the right and on reaching a track, turn right. Follow the track back to where you left the shorter route and turn left over the ladder stile.

* Head downhill, by a wall on the left. Climb another ladder stile, keep ahead to a waymarked post and continue down a sunken path to the next waymarked post. A brief detour to the left alongside a beck brings you to Lumb Spout.

Although only a small waterfall and occupying a secluded location, Lumb Spout used to attract many visitors in the past and even had a café nearby.

Return to the waymarked post and turn left to cross a footbridge over the beck. Walk along a track, go through a gate and keep ahead towards a farm. Go through a gate to the right of a fence. Pass to the right of the farm and continue along a track which emerges onto a narrow lane. Follow the lane downhill into the village of Trawden.

> ### REFRESHMENTS
>
> Visiting the only pub near the route, the Trawden Arms at Trawden, involves a brief detour. However, a wide choice of light meals – morning coffee, lunches, afternoon teas – is available in the pleasant surroundings of the Wycoller Craft Centre and Tearooms in the village (telephone: 01282 868395).

Trawden is a former mining and textile village. The tram tracks are all that is left of a route that opened in 1904 and finished in 1928. The rails were removed in 1942 to aid the war effort and the short stretch that is left is near the former tram terminus.

❹   By the bus terminus, bear right onto a cobbled track – this is where there is a stretch of old tram track – and by the gates of a bungalow on the left, turn right to a stile. (Keep ahead down the cobbled track if wanting to visit the pub in Trawden.) Climb the stile and head downhill along an enclosed path. Climb another stile at the bottom and continue downhill across a field to a footbridge over Trawden Brook. After crossing it, climb a stile and head uphill through a belt of trees to a farm. Go through a gate and keep ahead between the farm buildings to a track.

Continue along it and just after a cattle grid you reach a fingerpost at a crossways. Turn left along a path up to a gate, go through and keep ahead along the right edge of a field. Go through a gate in the corner and continue along a narrow enclosed path. Climb a stile, cross a track, go through another gate and keep ahead, passing in front of Little Laith Farm. Climb a stile, keep ahead towards the next farm. Climb another stile and keep by the right-hand field edge, passing to the left of the farm.

Continue along a track and where it bends right, keep ahead to a stile. Climb it and walk along the right edge of two fields to a kissing gate. After going through it, keep ahead across the next field to a stone stile. Climb it and head downhill through trees – there are steps in places – into the Wycoller valley. Go through a kissing gate, continue down steps to a tarmac track and turn left into Wycoller.

After turning right over the packhorse bridge, you pick up the outward route and retrace your steps uphill to the car park.

WALK 11
GLASSON DOCK AND THE CANAL AGE

Length: 8½ miles

The Lancaster Canal at Thurnham, which goes on to empty into the Lune estuary.

HOW TO GET THERE: Conder Green Picnic Site at the start of the walk is signposted from the A588, 1 mile east of Glasson Dock.

PARKING: At Conder Green Picnic Site.

MAP: OS Explorer 296 (Lancaster, Morecambe & Fleetwood) GR 456563.

INTRODUCTION

The flat and unspoilt countryside that borders the Lune estuary is ideal for this pleasant walk, and from the few slightly elevated points there are sweeping and extensive views across the estuary, Morecambe Bay and the Fylde. The line of the Bowland fells is always visible on the eastern horizon. As well as the Lancaster Canal basin at Glasson Dock, the walk is full of interest, including a disused railway, an old hall and the ruins of a medieval abbey, which reveals much of the history of this part of the Lancashire coast.

HISTORICAL BACKGROUND

Necessity is the mother of invention. The success of the Industrial Revolution created an urgent need for improvements in Britain's transport structure, especially the ability to get raw materials from their source to where industry required them and to move goods from their places of manufacture to the main ports.

Existing land transport was slow and inefficient. The roads were in a terrible state, virtually impassable during the winter months, and a journey from London to Manchester took between three and four days. It was often faster to go round the coasts and up the rivers, and small river ports flourished in the early days of industrial expansion. The problem was that many rivers were too small, not navigable and did not always go where they were most needed. The solution was to create artificial waterways, i.e. canals.

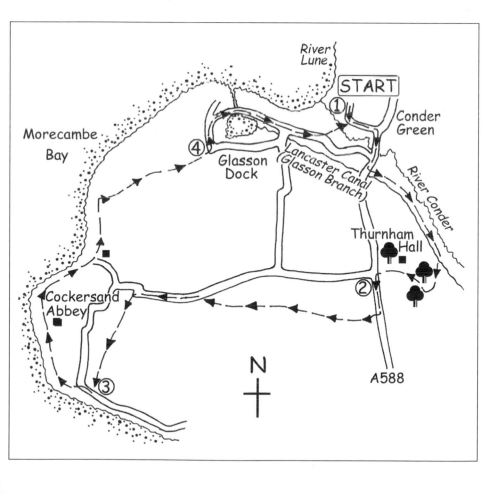

Although some canals had been built earlier in Britain, it was the construction of the Bridgewater Canal between 1759 and 1761 that really sparked off the great age of canal building. It was commissioned by the Duke of Bridgewater in order to transport coal from his mines at Worsley to the markets in Manchester. The engineer was James Brindley and he had to deal with huge and hitherto largely unknown constructional difficulties, such as taking the canal into the mine workings and carrying it over the River Irwell. The latter problem was brilliantly overcome by the building of an aqueduct. The canal was an immediate success and resulted in the halving of the price of coal in Manchester.

Over the next 50 to 60 years, local merchants and industrialists were encouraged to set up companies to construct similar canals, linking their areas with other parts of the country, and in particular with the major ports and river systems. Canal building reached its peak during the so-called 'Canal Mania' of the 1790s: in 1793 alone no fewer than 21 new canals were authorised.

Canals had their disadvantages. Although relatively inexpensive, they were still slow and the growth of railways after 1830, a much faster and more efficient form of transport, inevitably led to their decline. Unable to compete, their traffic dwindled and in time they were abandoned and neglected. After 1840 very few new ones were constructed, the notable exception being the Manchester Ship Canal in the 1890s.

By the end of the Second World War, many canals were in a very poor state but in the latter part of the 20th century they acquired a new lease of life, not as commercial waterways but – perhaps unexpectedly – as tourist attractions. They became centres for pleasure cruising and other recreational activities, such as walking and cycling. This resulted in the clearing and tidying up of banks and towpaths, repairing of locks and, to cater for the huge demand for boating facilities, the creation of marinas.

Nowhere are these welcome developments more obvious than on the Lancaster Canal, which for almost the whole of its length runs through highly attractive and unspoilt countryside.

THE WALK

❶   Begin by walking back to the main road by the Stork Hotel and turn right. Cross a bridge over the River Conder and in front of the canal bridge, turn left onto the canal towpath.

The Lancaster Canal was authorised in 1792 and completed in 1819. The engineer was John Rennie. It was built primarily to link Lancaster with Preston and the main cotton manufacturing centres further south. It also extended northwards to Kendal. The canal not only carried freight traffic but, from 1820 to 1846, the company ran a passenger service between Preston and Kendal, competing with the stagecoaches and offering customers tea, coffee and refreshments. The branch to Glasson Dock was completed in 1826 in order to connect the small port with the main canal network and to boost its prosperity.

Like many of the other canals throughout the country, the Lancaster Canal enjoyed a fairly brief heyday. It was badly affected by the opening of the railway line between Preston, Lancaster and Carlisle in the 1840s and subsequently sank into decline. Also like other canals, it has recently revived as a pleasure waterway and this may be further boosted by plans to reopen the northern stretch between Lancaster and Kendal, parts of which fell into disuse because they were blocked off by the construction of the M6 motorway in the 1960s.

Continue by the canal as far as the second bridge (no 4). After passing under it, turn right to cross a bridge by a lock and bear right to a stile. Climb it, bear left and head diagonally across a field to climb another stile in the far right corner. Keep ahead to cut across the corner of the next field. Climb a stile and keep ahead along the right-hand edge of a field, with Back Wood to the right. Climb a stile in front of Thurnham Roman Catholic church and turn right along a tarmac track. The track bends left and continues past Thurnham Hall to the A588.

Thurnham Hall was originally a small medieval pele tower. The present house was built in the 16th century and completely refaced in the 1820s in the contemporary Gothic Revival style. It was the home of the Thurnham family, who like many families in Lancashire suffered persecution after the Reformation for remaining loyal to the Catholic faith. Nowadays, it is a restaurant and country club.

❷ Turn left and, at a public footpath sign in front of a farm, turn right over a stile. Keep ahead and, after passing the corner of a wooden building, bear left across to the left-hand field edge. The way now continues along the left edge of a succession of fields, by a hedge on the left for most of the time and over a series of stiles and footbridges.

Eventually you cross a footbridge onto a lane and turn left. Where the lane bends right at a public footpath sign, turn left and walk along the left edge of fields, crossing several footbridges and with a ditch on the left. Look out for where you turn left to cross a footbridge over the ditch, and turn right to continue along right field edges. After going through two gates in quick succession, you emerge onto a lane by the shore of Morecambe Bay.

❸ From here to Glasson Dock you follow the Lancashire Coastal Way. Turn right and where the lane bends right, keep ahead along the sea wall, which follows the curve of the shore to the right to reach the scanty remains of Cockersand Abbey.

Cockersand Abbey occupies a lonely spot on this windswept coast overlooking the coastal marshes and wide expanses of Morecambe Bay. It was founded by William of Thurnham in 1184 and was inhabited by monks of the Premonstratensian Order. It was closed by Henry VIII in the 1530s and much of its stonework was used in later centuries for building the sea wall and providing a cheap and convenient quarry for local farmers. Little is left apart from the 13th-century octagonal chapter house, seen on the skyline earlier on the walk. This was preserved because it was used as the family mausoleum for the Daltons of Thurnham Hall.

Continue past the abbey ruins and the coast path later becomes a tarmac track. At a Lancashire Coastal Way sign in front of a farm, turn right and follow a winding track across fields, heading gently uphill to emerge onto a road at a bend.

❹ Turn left to reach a superb viewpoint over Glasson Dock and the Lune estuary.

A viewfinder beside the road indicates all the places that are visible from here in clear conditions. They include Blackpool Tower, some of the Lakeland and Pennine peaks and, nearer at hand, Lancaster Castle, the buildings of Lancaster University and Heysham Power Station. Just on the other side of the River Lune, the row of houses at Sunderland Point can be seen. In many ways Sunderland Point was the predecessor of Glasson Dock; an earlier attempt to develop a port on the Lune estuary in order to maintain Lancaster's trade.

Glasson Dock, where the canal empties into the Lune estuary.

At the viewpoint, turn right along Tithebarn Lane to Glasson Dock.

The new port of Glasson Dock on the south side of the Lune estuary was founded in 1787 in order to safeguard the prosperity of the port of Lancaster. Lancaster had flourished throughout the 18th century but its future was threatened by the silting up of the river. An earlier attempt to counteract this problem was the creation of Sunderland Point on the north side of the river but this was not a success.

> ### REFRESHMENTS
>
> The Stork Hotel at Conder Green does a wide variety of meals to suit all tastes, appetites and pockets, in a most attractive and atmospheric setting. The inn has been around for a long time: a board in the bar lists the names of all the landlords since the 17th century (telephone: 01524 751234). In addition, you pass the Thurnham Mill Hotel and Restaurant beside the canal and there are pubs and cafés at Glasson Dock.

Despite strenuous attempts to make it a going concern, Glasson Dock was only marginally more successful. The silting up of the river was only part of the problems facing the future of Lancaster and the Lune estuary ports. The area was too far away from the main centres of industry and population in south Lancashire and there was also competition from other Irish Sea ports, such as Whitehaven, Heysham and Preston. Attempts to solve the communications problem, first by constructing the canal link with the main Lancaster Canal and secondly by building the rail link with Lancaster and the main west coast route, were of no avail and Glasson Dock and commercial traffic on the Lune continued to decline.

It is still a port but nowadays it mainly operates as a centre for pleasure boating and it has a popular and successful marina.

Cross the canal to a T-junction and turn right. Just beyond the Victoria Hotel, bear left onto the Lune Estuary Footpath.

The Lune Estuary Footpath uses the track of a former single-line railway from Lancaster to Glasson Dock that was built by the London and North Western Railway Company. It opened in 1883, passenger traffic ceased in the 1930s and it finally closed down in 1962. Like the canal, it was built to link Glasson Dock with the main transport network and thus boost its development as a commercial port. Also like the canal, it largely failed in this respect.

Follow the footpath back to the starting point.

WALK 12

RUFFORD OLD HALL AND THE AGRICULTURAL REVOLUTION

Length: 5½ miles

Rufford Old Hall.

HOW TO GET THERE: Mere Sands Wood Nature Reserve is just off the B5246 about 1 mile west of Rufford.

PARKING: There is a car park at Mere Sands Wood.

MAP: OS Explorer 285 (Southport & Chorley) GR 447159.

INTRODUCTION

The attractive woodland and meres of the nature reserve are a delight to explore at both the start and end of the walk. In between, the route takes you along the towpath of the Leeds and Liverpool Canal, from where there are extensive views across the wide, open and intensively farmed expanses of the West Lancashire coast plain to the western fringes of the Pennines, and past Rufford Old Hall, a medieval black and white manor house, once owned by the family who created this rich agricultural land from a boggy marsh.

HISTORICAL BACKGROUND

In the 18th and 19th centuries there was an agricultural as well as an industrial revolution. The two events were closely linked: the rise in population created an increased demand for food and therefore a need for more efficient farming and the more efficient farming released labourers for the fast expanding industries.

Compared with many other parts of the country, Lancashire was a relatively unproductive county and in west Lancashire the greatest obstacles to improve-

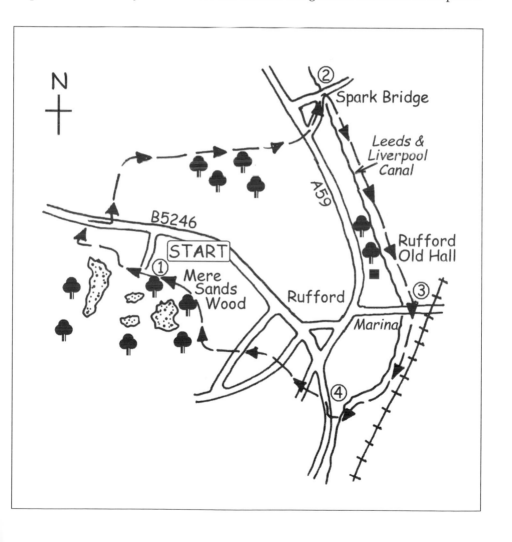

ment and increased crop production were the huge undrained marshes and mosses, such as Martin Mere and Chat Moss that covered much of the area. One of the main problems in draining these large areas was the enormous investment required, an investment only worthwhile if the capital, markets and transport were available.

By the middle of the 19th century most of these criteria were in place. First canals and then railways had improved transport and communications in the region, which meant that farmers could get their produce to the local markets. The huge rise in population in the nearby mining and textile districts created the markets, and many of the more enterprising landowners had amassed capital from becoming involved in local industrial and building projects.

Before it was drained, Martin Mere covered much of the area between Rufford and the sea and Ribble estuary, nearly 4 miles long and 2 miles wide. The present Martin Mere, now a wildfowl and wetlands centre, is but a fraction of its original size. Ownership was divided between the Heskeths of Rufford and other local landowners. Attempts at drainage were made in the late 17th century and again in the late 18th century but these were largely unsuccessful, partly through natural reasons and partly because of opposition and sabotage from local farmers who wanted to protect their irrigation rights.

During the 19th century Sir Thomas Hesketh and other landowners persevered with more success. Drainage schemes were inaugurated around Rufford and Croston about 1800 and penalties were imposed on people who deliberately broke down banks to cause flooding. By 1850 a complex system of drains and the use of steam-powered pumps had enabled the Heskeths to successfully drain their share of the mere and about 800 acres of extra land were brought into cultivation. This had the effect of virtually draining the whole of the mere, creating a huge new area of rich and fertile land. Thus, the Heskeths were among the pioneers and driving forces behind a movement which transformed a formerly barren and waterlogged area into a major vegetable growing region.

THE WALK

Mere Sands Wood was planted by the Hesketh family in about the middle of the 19th century. It comprises around 105 acres (42 hectares) of woodland, heath, meadow and small meres and was originally an area of sand and peat on the edge of a large lake. Between 1974 and 1982 it was extensively quarried for sand and the meres were formed from the extracted areas. Subsequent restoration has resulted in a popular and nationally important nature reserve, with a wide range of wildlife and habitats.

The reserve is owned and managed by the Wildlife Trust of Lancashire, Manchester and North Merseyside. Visitors are invited to walk the various colour-coded trails, observe the wildlife from several hides scattered around the reserve and to take a look around the visitor centre. Admission is free but as the Wildlife Trust depends entirely on donations, membership fees and grants, a donation is greatly appreciated.

❶ From the car park, take the blue-waymarked path through the trees. The path bends first right and then left to continue along the right inside edge of the wood. At a footpath sign to Holmeswood village, turn right. Cross a footbridge – here leaving the nature reserve – and keep ahead along the left edge of a field to a road. Turn right and, at a public footpath sign, turn left along a tarmac track, passing to the right of a bungalow. Where the tarmac ends, keep ahead along a straight, grassy track across fields to a T-junction. Turn right and at a crossways, keep ahead along a tarmac track. In front of a gate, turn left alongside a fence on the right, curving right to rejoin the tarmac track, and bear left to continue along it to a road. Cross over and take the lane opposite (Spark Lane) which curves left to a T-junction.

❷ Turn right over Spark Bridge and immediately turn left through a hedge gap. Descend steps to the towpath of the Leeds and Liverpool Canal and turn left to pass under the bridge.

The Leeds and Liverpool Canal was constructed between 1770 and 1816 to allow trade across the Pennines between the woollen industries of Yorkshire and the cotton industries of Lancashire. In particular, it was built to give Leeds and the surrounding areas of Yorkshire access to the port of Liverpool. It is 127 miles long, making it the longest single canal in Britain.

This stretch of the canal is the Rufford Branch or Douglas Navigation. It was built to provide a link between the main canal and the Ribble estuary and for the most part runs parallel with the River Douglas, which it joins at Tarleton.

Continue along the towpath and just after passing a swing bridge, the grounds of Rufford Old Hall can be seen on the other side of the canal. Later the house itself comes into view and shortly afterwards the path gently ascends to the road at Rufford.

❸ In order to visit the hall, turn right over the canal bridge, passing Rufford's 19th-century church, and at a T-junction, turn right along the main road to the entrance.

Rufford Old Hall is an outstanding example of a late medieval, black and white manor house. Such houses were common throughout west Lancashire and Cheshire because of the shortage of local building stone and abundance of timber.

It was built by the Heskeths in the late 15th and early 16th centuries as a timber-framed structure on a stone base. At the time of the Reformation, the Heskeths were one of many Lancashire families who rejected Protestantism and stayed true to the Catholic church. A brick extension was added to the house in 1662 and another extension was built in the early 19th century. Around the middle of the 18th century, the Heskeths moved out of the old hall into a new and more spacious one in another part of their estate – now on the other side of the A59.

Rufford's most outstanding feature is the great hall, built between 1463 and 1490 and noted for its magnificent hammerbeam roof and ornate moveable screen. Throughout the house there are fine collections of antique furniture, paintings, ceramics and armour and – to be expected in a Catholic house – a

REFRESHMENTS

You can choose from the Rufford Arms near Spark Bridge, a café at Fettlers Wharf Marina at Rufford, a tearoom at Rufford Old Hall and a drinks machine at Mere Sands Wood Visitor Centre! Fettlers Wharf Marina Tearoom and Restaurant does a variety of meals – cooked lunches, light snacks and teas – in a delightful setting. In fine weather you can sit outdoors at picnic tables overlooking the marina (telephone: 01704 822888).

priest's hiding place. Meadows, woodland and ornamental gardens lead down to the banks of the Leeds and Liverpool Canal and provide an attractive setting. In 1936 the house was given to the National Trust.

For details of opening times and admission charges, telephone 01704 821254.

Return to the bridge over the canal and turn right to rejoin the towpath, passing to the right of Fettlers Wharf Marina. Turn right over the first bridge – a swing bridge – to a road and turn right again.

❹ At a public footpath sign, turn left down steps and walk along the left bank of the Rufford Boundary Sluice. Continue beside it, crossing it and recrossing it three times at a succession of roads. Finally, walk along its right bank, by the edge of a cricket field, to a kissing gate in a field corner. Go through, here re-entering the woodlands of the nature reserve. Turn right along the right-hand inside edge of the trees and the path leads back to the start.

WALK 13

LEIGHTON HALL AND THE ENGLISH COUNTRY HOUSE

Length: 6 miles

Leighton Hall, near the shores of Morecambe Bay.

HOW TO GET THERE: The walk starts at Eaves Wood car park (National Trust), about 1 mile north-east of Silverdale village and just over ½ mile north of Silverdale station.

PARKING: Eaves Wood car park.

MAP: OS Explorer OL7 (The English Lakes – South Eastern area) GR 472759

INTRODUCTION

This is a walk of great variety and much attractive scenery in the Arnside-Silverdale Area of Outstanding Natural Beauty in the far north-west corner of Lancashire, close to the Cumbrian border. The extensive views take in the outline of the southern fells of the Lake District and the wide sweep of Morecambe Bay.

As well as Leighton Hall, a great country house occupied by the Gillow family since 1822, the walk embraces both a nature reserve and the RSPB reserve at Leighton Moss, and much attractive woodland. All the paths are clear, well-signed and easy to follow.

HISTORICAL BACKGROUND

The 18th and 19th centuries were the heyday of the stately homes of England and the people who owned and resided in them. For over 200 years, from the late 17th century up to the outbreak of the First World War, the English aristocracy reigned supreme, dominating all aspects of social and political life. Their houses naturally varied quite considerably in size, according to the wealth of the individual owner. Some were on quite a modest scale; others were grand and opulent. In their palatial country houses, surrounded by ornamental gardens and sweeping parkland, the aristocracy were the owners of all they could survey from their windows and terraces and these houses were the scene of many glittering social occasions.

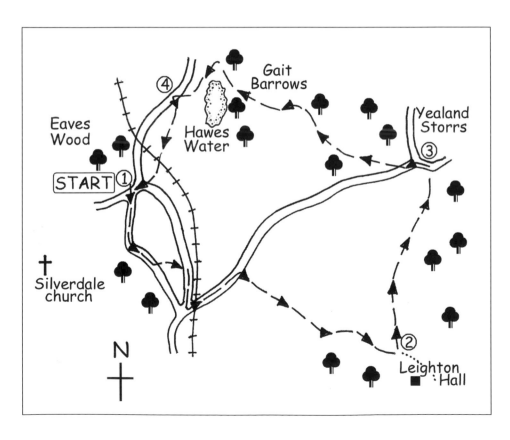

Before the Industrial Revolution, Lancashire had been one of the poorer and more sparsely populated counties in England and therefore its country houses tended to be modest. Here there were no grand mansions on the scale of Chatsworth, Blenheim, or Castle Howard. Most of Lancashire's country houses were relatively small manor houses rather than palatial residences. The grandest houses were to be found in the south of the county, for example, Knowsley, home of the Earls of Derby, and Croxteth Hall, owned by the Earls of Sefton.

Some landowners became even wealthier as a result of the Industrial Revolution, especially those in the North and Midlands who had mineral resources on their land, which they exploited enthusiastically. But generally the 19th century saw a gradual shift in the balance of power, with the dominance of the landowners being gradually usurped by the rise of the middle class industrialists. It is noteworthy that two of the most outstanding Victorian prime ministers – Sir Robert Peel and William Gladstone – sprang from the Lancashire industrial class, Peel from Bury and Gladstone from Liverpool, rather than from the traditional aristocracy.

Leighton Hall is a country house that illustrates this transition. It had previously been owned by a succession of aristocratic families but in the early 19th century it was purchased by the Gillows, who had a furniture-making business in Lancaster. The same family still owns it today.

The decline of the English country house was a slow process. Apart from the Industrial Revolution, two major factors were the growth of democracy – universal suffrage was virtually complete by 1918 and affected the political power of the landowners – and the imposition of death duties. The two world wars made matters worse. During the Second World War many country houses were requisitioned by the army and by 1945 they were in a generally bad state. One solution, increasingly widespread since the end of the Second World War, was to open them up to the general public. This has enabled many – including Leighton Hall – to be maintained, lived in by the same family and to display their treasures, both inside and outside, for all to enjoy and appreciate.

THE WALK

❶ Exit the car park and walk along the lane opposite (The Row), passing an ancient natural pond that has been recently restored.

The tower of Silverdale's 19th-century church can be seen over to the right. In the Victorian era this formerly remote and scattered hamlet on the shores of Morecambe Bay developed into a small holiday resort, especially after the building of the Furness Railway between Lancaster and Barrow made it more accessible. The village makes an excellent walking centre, with cliffs, limestone outcrops and extensive woodlands in the vicinity and a network of public footpaths radiating from it.

At a public footpath sign to 'Railway Station', turn left through a kissing gate and take a clearly marked path across part of Silverdale golf course, heading down to a stone stile. Climb it and turn right along a road, passing Silverdale station. Take the first road on the left, signposted to Yealand Redmayne and Kendal.

Almost immediately you pass the Leighton Moss Nature Reserve car park and visitor centre. Continue past it for about 300 yards and at a public bridleway sign to Leighton Hall Farm and a public footpath sign to Yealand Conyers, turn right along a straight track which takes you across the nature reserve.

The RSPB's popular nature reserve at Leighton Moss, situated on the shores of Morecambe Bay, comprises a variety of habitats: lagoons, reed beds – including the largest in north-west England – and woodland. Among the wildfowl and wading birds that are attracted here are such rare species as bitterns, bearded tits and marsh harriers. There are nature trails and public hides from which to observe the wildlife and the visitor centre has interesting displays, a shop and tearoom (telephone: 01524 701601).

After going through a gate on the far side, the track winds gently uphill and passes between houses – it now becomes a tarmac track – to reach a public footpath sign to Yealand Storrs.

❷ The main route continues to the left here but keep ahead along the track to the entrance to Leighton Hall, about 300 yards further on.

Leighton Hall was originally a medieval manor house, dating back to at least the 13th century. Unlike some houses which have been owned by just one family throughout their history, Leighton has had a succession of owners. In the 18th century it came into the possession of the Towneley family of Towneley Hall, near Burnley. George Towneley built a new Georgian house – the old one had been partially destroyed during the Jacobite rebellion of 1715 – and laid out the park in 1763. In 1822 the house passed to its present owners, the Gillows, the well-known family of furniture manufacturers from nearby Lancaster.

The early 19th century was the era of the Gothic Revival and Richard Gillow gave the house its Gothic appearance by re-facing it in pale grey limestone. His son added to it by building a tower and a new wing in 1870.

Leighton Hall is still occupied by the Gillows and inside the rooms have a pleasantly informal and lived in atmosphere. As might be expected, there is a lot of Gillow furniture on display as well as some fine paintings. The gardens are attractive and from the sloping parkland there are magnificent views of the Lakeland fells. An unusual feature is a collection of birds of prey.

For details of opening times and admission charges, telephone 01524 734474.

Return to the public footpath sign to Yealand Storrs (point 2) and turn right through a gate onto a track. The way is now across or along the edge of a succession of fields and through a series of gates. Finally, where the wall on the left bears left, keep ahead past a waymarked post and bear left by a wall on the right to reach a gate. Go through and keep ahead to climb a stone stile onto a road.

❸ Turn left and, where the road forks, go through a gate between the two forks and take the path ahead through the woodland of Yealand Hall Allotment.

Gaps in the trees on the left reveal fine views over Morecambe Bay.

Keep ahead through the wood, going through two gates, and immediately after the second one you come to a T-junction. Turn left to continue along the left inside edge of the trees. Just before reaching a gate in front, look out for where you turn left through a narrow gate and walk across a field to a fingerpost. Turn right through a gate and squeezer stile to enter the National Nature Reserve of Gait Barrows.

Gait Barrows covers 301 acres (121 hectares) and is managed by English Nature. Its varied and attractive terrain contains some of the most important limestone pavements in the country, as well as woodland and the tree-fringed lake of Hawes Water.

Walk across a field, cross a low wall and head gently downhill across the next field, making for the far right corner. Go through a kissing gate to enter the woodland bordering Hawes Water. Turn right, cross a plank causeway and continue through the trees. The path curves left and heads uphill to emerge, via a gate, onto a road.

❹ Turn left, and turn left again at the side of a large house – there is a public footpath sign to Red Bridge. Go through a gate and walk along a track to a stile. Climb it and take the path ahead across a field, which curves right, passes a redundant gatepost and continues to another stile. After climbing it, keep ahead across the next field. Climb a stile on the far side. Carefully cross the railway line, climb another stile and continue along the right edge of a field. Climb a stile onto a road. Turn right and where the road bends right, keep ahead along Park Road to the start.

WALK 14

BLACKPOOL TOWER AND THE VICTORIAN SEASIDE RESORT

Length: 8 miles

Looking across Marton Mere towards Blackpool Tower.

HOW TO GET THERE: The walk begins on the Promenade in front of Blackpool Tower.

PARKING: There are a number of pay-and-display car parks in the centre of Blackpool.

MAP: OS Explorer 286 (Blackpool & Preston) GR 305361.

INTRODUCTION

This walk takes you surprisingly quickly and easily from the urban surroundings of Blackpool Promenade into the sylvan delights of Stanley Park and then on to the tranquil rural landscapes around Marton Mere. There are attractive views across the countryside of the Fylde and from many points on the route, the unmistakeable landmark of the Tower can be seen on the horizon.

HISTORICAL BACKGROUND

The growth of large holiday resorts around the British coastline is very much a Victorian phenomenon. Before that, holidays were the preserve of the rich and, in the main, they were cultural events. Towards the end of the 18th century, however, some towns on the south coast were becoming fashionable and sea bathing was starting to become popular as it was believed to have health giving properties. Brighton, in particular, ideally situated not too far from London, was boosted by the visits of the Prince Regent and his building of the spectacular Oriental-style Royal Pavilion.

Blackpool was a relative newcomer in the holiday resort stakes. It lacked both the scenic and climatic advantages of the south coast resorts, as well as their affluence. It could not even compete with their northern counterpart of Scarborough, with its picturesque castle ruins, sandy bays and grand cliff scenery. Even as late as 1840, Blackpool was little more than a scattered collection of houses on the flat, windy and marshy Fylde coast, with a population of only around 1,000. By the end of the 19th century this had grown to 47,000, and to 106,000 in 1931.

Railways were the biggest single factor in the growth of the Victorian seaside resort, and nowhere more so than Blackpool. The Lancashire and Yorkshire Railway arrived in 1846, linking Blackpool with the outside world and especially with the rapidly expanding textile manufacturing and coal mining towns of Lancashire and Yorkshire. A combination of cheap fares, regular employment and relative proximity to these industrial areas led to a mass

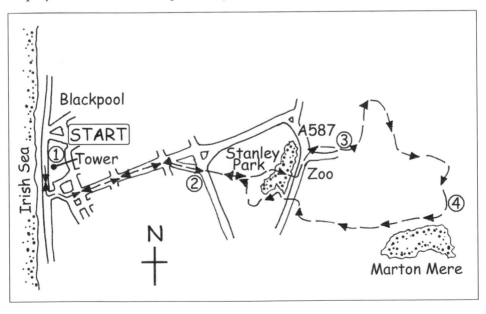

Blackpool Tower.

influx of mainly working class visitors. By the 1860s the visitors, both day trippers and those who stayed in the resort, totalled around 25,000 and by 1914 this had risen to nearly 4 million. They came for sand, sea, fresh air, fun and entertainment. Nature provided the first three, Blackpool set out in earnest to provide the latter two.

Although there were more genteel middle class areas towards the north and south ends of the sea front, from the start Blackpool was unashamedly the supreme working class resort. Between 1870 and 1914 it built a succession of amenities and 'entertainment palaces' to cater for the needs of its army of visitors. A new promenade was built in 1870, the Winter Gardens opened in 1878 followed by the Opera House in 1889 and, most daring and famous of all, Blackpool Tower rose above the town in 1894. In addition, there were other theatres and ballrooms, piers and a funfair. The renowned illuminations made their debut before the First World War but did not become fully operational until 1925. They were – and still are – a phenomenal success and prolong Blackpool's holiday season until well into November.

Despite depression and unemployment in the northern industrial towns after the First World War, Blackpool reached the peak of its popularity in the 1920s and 1930s, with the largest visitor numbers and the longest season of any British resort. It continued to flourish in the years after the ending of the Second World War until changing tastes, the advent of cheap package tours and the attraction of guaranteed sunshine tempted many of its potential visitors elsewhere.

It still draws the crowds, still puts on a good show and is currently seeking to partially re-invent itself as a British Las Vegas. Will it succeed? Who knows, but it will have a good try!

THE WALK

Blackpool Tower has become the undisputed symbol of the town, much as the Eiffel Tower is the symbol of Paris. The inspiration for it came from the latter as Blackpool decided to cash in on its fast growing popularity by building its own version of the Eiffel Tower in 1890. As was to be expected, such an audacious and ambitious scheme had its critics within the town but their criticisms were overcome. Blackpool Tower Company was set up in 1891, the money for the venture was raised, work commenced and the Tower opened in 1894.

It contained the famous ballroom, a concert hall, circus, zoo, aquarium and roof garden. The Tower rose 518 feet above the Promenade and town, and from such dizzy heights, its intrepid visitors could get stunning – and for some, terrifying – views over the town, the Fylde countryside and the Irish Sea. With its combination of boldness and brashness and variety of indoor entertainments, it was a great success. Right from the start the holidaymakers poured in, especially at those times when the Blackpool weather turned fickle, and they have been doing so ever since. For details of opening times, telephone 01253 292029.

❶ Start by facing the Tower and turn right along the Promenade towards Central Pier. Turn left into New Bonny Street. At a T-junction turn right and then turn left along Hornby Road. After ¾ mile bear right along Mere Road, which brings you to the entrance to Stanley Park.

❷ Walk along a straight, tree-lined tarmac track through the park. Keep ahead at a junction of tracks, passing to the right of the café, and continue along the left edge of the park lake.

The beautifully landscaped Stanley Park was opened in 1926 and its quiet pleasures provide visitors with a sometimes welcome alternative to the more raucous entertainments on the Golden Mile. It has a boating lake, colourful flower beds, tennis, bowling, pitch and putt and a model village. Pride of place goes to the superb Italian Gardens, well worth a close inspection. Adjacent to the park there is quite a variety of amenities. These include a sports centre, cricket ground and Blackpool zoo. For details of opening times, telephone 01253 478428.

Bear right to cross a bridge. Walk across a small wooded island in the lake and cross another bridge to emerge onto a road. Cross over, turn left – the zoo is on the right – and then turn right along Woodside Drive. Almost immediately turn left through an arch into Salisbury Gardens, an area of woodland. Before reaching a footbridge over a brook, turn right onto a winding path and continue through the trees. There are lots of paths here but you simply need to keep to the right of the brook and eventually you emerge onto a tarmac drive.

❸ Climb the stile opposite and at a footpath sign ahead, bear right through a gap in a fence onto a path which heads gently uphill to another footpath sign.
    Bear left, in the Newton Drive direction, and follow a path which curves right around the left-hand edge of a golf course, with a parallel path and cycleway on the left all the while. At a public footpath sign, where a path across the golf course comes in from the right, turn left to continue by the left edge of the course. Again the path curves right.

The views across the golf course are surprisingly rural and Blackpool Tower stands out clearly on the horizon.

❹ The next change of direction is not easy to pinpoint as it is not signed. Where the path does a right bend – this is just after passing the corner of a small pool from where you get a particularly fine view of the Tower – head over to the parallel cycleway on the left and look out for a clear path that leads off through trees. Walk along it and about 50 yards after going through a kissing gate, turn right to a T-junction. Turn right again along a path parallel to the north side of Marton Mere.

Marton Mere comprises water, reedbeds, scrub and grassland. It was originally much larger than its present size, over 3 miles in length, around 1¹/₂ miles wide and surrounded by marsh and dunes. Successive drainage schemes and a build-up of sediment have been the main reasons for its drastic shrinkage and the area around it has been reclaimed for agriculture and become more built up. Despite the growth of Blackpool's suburbs, it is still a pleasant and tranquil spot, popular with walkers, anglers and bird watchers.

Interestingly it was from the black, peat-stained waters of the mere that Blackpool acquired its name.

At the end of the path go through a kissing gate and turn right along the left-hand one of two paths ahead. Go through a kissing gate and, at a T-junction ahead, turn left, in the direction of Stanley Park. The path curves right and, on reaching the tarmac drive to the Herons Gate Hotel, turn left to a road.

Cross over, turn left and almost immediately turn right onto a tarmac drive to re-enter Stanley Park. At a crossways, turn right to keep alongside the lake. Just before the bandstand, turn sharp left onto a path which curves right. Keep ahead at another crossways. At the next signpost, turn right and at the clock tower turn right again through the Italian Gardens up to the front of the café.

Turn left, here rejoining the outward route, and retrace your steps along Mere Road and Hornby Road to Blackpool Tower.

> **REFRESHMENTS**
>
> There are plenty of pubs, cafés and fish and chip shops in Blackpool and an excellent licensed café in Stanley Park. This café, built in the Art Deco style and overlooking the Italian Gardens, offers a wide variety of lunches and light meals, together with a superb selection of ice creams. It also has a cheese stall and rock shop (telephone: 01253 694604).

Walk 15

Helmshore Textile Museums and 'King Cotton'

Length: 5½ miles

The 18th-century Higher Mill at Helmshore Textile Museum.

HOW TO GET THERE: Helmshore Textile Museums are on the B6235 about 1½ miles south-west of Haslingden and signposted from the A56.

PARKING: There is a car park at the Helmshore Textile Museums.

MAP: OS Explorer 287 (West Pennine Moors) GR 777215.

Introduction

The cotton industry is indelibly associated with Lancashire during the Industrial Revolution and the Helmshore Textile Museums offer a fascinating insight into the heyday of 'King Cotton'. The walk then takes you across an area of open moorland, part of the Forest of Rossendale. Although surrounded by industries, large towns and busy roads, these moors retain their largely wild and unspoilt atmosphere and you are hardly aware of industrial activity and urban growth, apart from distant views into the valley bottoms and when walking through a disused quarry. There is some climbing and rough moorland walking, plus one steep descent near the end.

HISTORICAL BACKGROUND

Until the 18th century the main industries in Lancashire were wool, farming and quarrying. It was then that cotton manufacture started to expand rapidly and by the early 19th century it dominated the Lancashire textile industry, having almost totally replaced wool and linen. It was the cotton industry that pioneered many of the major developments of the Industrial Revolution, leading the way both in the introduction of new machinery and in the growth of working in mills and factories instead of – as previously – at home.

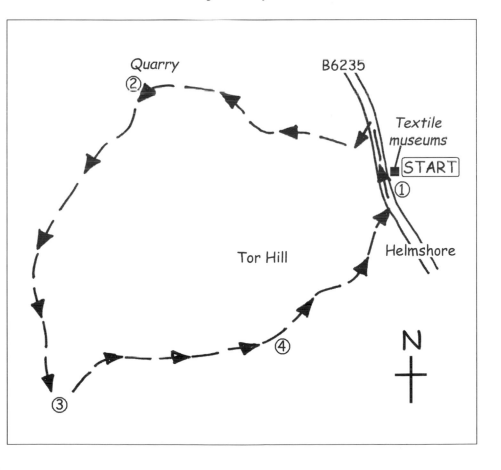

The heyday of cotton was from around 1850 to the outbreak of the First World War. Lancashire had virtually no competition at the time and totally dominated world markets. Although there was increasing competition from abroad from the 1870s onwards, plus periods of depression and bouts of labour unrest, this was an era of great prosperity and Lancashire's domination of world output and trade continued. Britain's share of the world trade in cotton peaked at a staggering 82% in 1882 and was still 58% in 1910-13. In 1886 an observer noted: 'There is scarcely a nook or corner in the habitable globe where the products of the spindles and looms of Lancashire do not find a market.'

The statistics tell their own story. In 1911 the cotton industry overall employed over 1½ million people, most of whom lived and worked in Lancashire. Many of them were women – three women to every two men – and over 10% of the workforce were children. The latter were both cheap and available and particularly useful in smaller towns and rural areas where there was sometimes a shortage of labour. At this time, cotton was the largest single export industry and by 1850 it accounted for around 40% of British exports. Despite the rise of other industries, increasing foreign competition and the depression of 1873-96, it still accounted for about 25% on the eve of the First World War.

The First World War had a devastating effect, not just on the fortunes of cotton but on all the other staple industries of 19th-century Britain: wool, coal, shipbuilding and engineering. The war cut Britain off from most of her export markets and once these were lost, they were difficult to regain, especially as their loss coincided with the acceleration of foreign competition. The Lancashire cotton industry was particularly badly affected by competition from the Far East. The huge cost of the war meant that there was a shortage of money in the post-war world and this led to the further decline of markets. In addition, there had been little incentive or desire for the Lancashire cotton manufacturers to modernise when they had been cushioned by guaranteed prosperity in the good times and this meant that in the new, harsher post-war world the industry was somewhat backward compared with its newer competitors.

This combination of factors led to a severe slump in the inter-war years, at its worst in the early 1930s. Since then, apart from a few short periods of recovery, noticeably during the Second World War, the decline has continued and cotton is now a minor industry.

Some of the proud and impressive mill buildings that were erected in the heyday of cotton have survived, though, including Horrocksfords in Preston (1895) and India Mill at Darwen (1913). Nowadays they are mostly put to a variety of uses, serving other industries, converted into homes, or – as in the case of those at Helmshore – used as museums.

There is one truly amazing statistic regarding the era when cotton was king, revealed when looking around the museums. At its peak just before the outbreak of the First World War, Lancashire produced approximately 7 million km of cloth, enough to wrap around the earth 180 times or to stretch 18 times between the earth and the moon.

THE WALK

There are two textile museums at Helmshore, housed in separate but adjoining mill buildings. The smaller building, Higher Mill, was a late 18th-century woollen fulling mill, one of the earliest in Rossendale, built by the Turner family in 1789. Fulling was a process that involved the cleansing and stretching of the woollen cloth. The cloth was cleansed by soaking it in human urine – collected from the local farms at a penny a barrel – and then pounded by fulling hammers powered by a water wheel, still operating today and an impressive sight.

The larger building, Whitaker's Mill, was built in the early 19th century as a cotton spinning mill. Although named after a later owner, it also was built by a member of the Turner family, William Turner, and was powered by steam. It had to be rebuilt after a disastrous fire in 1859-60. Inside a series of displays tell you the history of the Lancashire cotton industry – its origins, rise and fall, social conditions of the workers and the growth of the nearby cotton towns. There are interesting interactive activities and the museum puts on regular demonstrations of working machinery.

A leisurely walk around these two mills is a fascinating experience and really does transport you back to the days of the Industrial Revolution when Great Britain was 'the workshop of the world' and Lancashire cotton was king. For details of opening times and admission charges, telephone 01706 226459.

❶ Turn right out of the car park, along the road. At a public footpath sign to Musbury Heights, turn sharp left along a tarmac track which heads uphill behind a row of cottages. The track continues steadily uphill and bends right to a stile. Climb it and continue along a rough track. After the next stile, turn right, first along an enclosed track and then along a walled path, climbing several stiles. Head up an embankment to join a track and, where the track bends right, keep ahead to a gate. Go through and at a fork ahead, take the right-hand track which heads up through the remains of a disused quarry to climb a stile.

The quarry ahead and the reservoirs seen over to the right indicate that there was more to Rossendale than just textiles. Other economic uses included serving as a water catchment area, especially useful after the growth of large towns in the locality, and Rossendale flagstone was much in demand to pave the streets of many towns and cities of Victorian England, including London.

❷ Just in front of a small ruined stone building, turn sharp left onto a path which passes between the spoil heaps of the quarry to a stone stile. Climb it – you

are now on the Rossendale Way – and
follow a path across open moorland,
contouring along the side of the valley,
fording streams, passing ruined farms
and climbing several stiles.

*In the Middle Ages, the Forest of Rossen-
dale was part of the estates belonging to
the De Lacys of Clitheroe Castle. This part of the walk is across the former Musbury
Park, enclosed from the forest as a deer park in 1305 by Henry de Lacy.*

The path curves gradually left around the head of the valley.

❸ Immediately after fording a stream, there is a definite left turn and you
continue back along the other side of the valley. The path bends left, between a
wall on the right and a wire fence on the left, to a kissing gate. Go through it,
climb two stiles in quick succession and after the second one, turn right along the
right-hand edge of a field. After about 50 yards, bear left and walk across the field
to a gate. Go through and keep ahead along a track, passing to the left of a copse
and later keeping by a wall on the right, to a kissing gate. Go through and walk
down a concrete farm track.

❹ In front of a gate, bear left – here leaving the Rossendale Way – along a
grassy path by a wall on the right. Climb a stone stile and continue by the wall
on the right, heading down to a public footpath sign in the field corner. Climb
the stile in front and turn right along the right-hand edge of the next field to a
stile. Climb it, keep ahead to climb another stile and continue along a track
which bends left.

Where the track bends right, keep ahead over a stone stile and walk along a
right-hand field edge. Climb a stile and continue along the right edge of the
next field. When you see the museum buildings below in the valley, bear
slightly left away from the field edge towards them. A steep descent leads to a
stile. Turn right over it and follow a walled track downhill to a tarmac drive and
onto a road. Turn left to return to the start.

Walk 16
Rivington and a Victorian Philanthropist

Length: 5 miles

Great House Barn at Rivington.

HOW TO GET THERE: Rivington Country Park, Great House Barn, is about ½ mile to the south of Rivington village, which is on the minor road between Belmont and Adlington.

PARKING: At Great House Barn.

MAP: OS Explorer 287 (West Pennine Moors) GR 628138.

Introduction

Rivington Country Park is based around Lever Park, created in the early years of the 20th century by Lord Leverhulme as a public recreation area for the people of Bolton. This interesting walk visits all the main historic features of the park – the two Saxon barns, the 18th-century hall, the reservoirs and mock castle ruins – and also embraces its varied terrain: woodland, lakeshore, grassland and open moorland. From the higher points – the Pigeon Tower, terraced gardens and especially the summit of Rivington Pike – the views are tremendous.

HISTORICAL BACKGROUND

Lord Leverhulme was one of the foremost enlightened and philanthropic employers of the Victorian era. Born William Hesketh Lever in Bolton in 1851, he leased a small soapworks in Warrington while still quite a young man and soon built up a successful and thriving business.

As his business flourished, he established a new factory at Port Sunlight on the Wirral and built a model estate there for his workforce. In 1900, by now a millionaire, he bought the Rivington estate for himself and decided to convert it into a public park, to be called Lever Park, for the people of his home town. Thousands of trees were planted, broad drives were constructed, the two ancient barns in the area were restored and a replica of the medieval ruins of Liverpool Castle was built on a promontory above Lower Rivington reservoir.

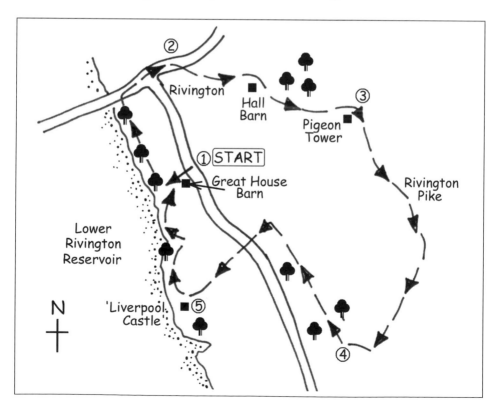

On the steep hillside above the park, he built himself a bungalow and laid out ornamental terraced gardens in the Japanese style, with lakes, cascades, fountains and various structures. The bungalow was burnt down in 1913 and later rebuilt but after Lord Leverhulme's death in 1925, it fell into ruin and had to be demolished. The gardens were neglected and subsequently became a wilderness.

After the park was designated a country park the work of restoration began. Although the terraced gardens have never been brought back to their original splendour, the park has been made attractive again and the whole area is now fully available for the enjoyment and recreation of the general public, thus fulfilling the intentions of its founder.

THE WALK

Both Great House Barn and Hall Barn – the latter about ½ mile away – are reputed to be of Saxon origin, though extensive restoration, partly by Lord Leverhulme, has given them more of a Victorian than a Saxon or even Tudor appearance. Great House Barn was once much larger than now but both barns are impressive by their sheer size alone. Hall Barn is a pub and restaurant and Great House Barn is used as a café, gift shop and information centre (telephone: 01204 691549).

❶ With your back to the barn, take the public bridleway that leads off from the end of the car park towards the reservoir.

The reservoirs – this one, Lower Rivington, and the adjacent Upper Rivington, Yarrow and Anglezarke reservoirs – were constructed in the middle of the 19th century to provide water for the city of Liverpool. They are now maintained by United Utilities.

On reaching a track, turn right and follow it through woodland and on through a car park to a road. Turn right into Rivington, passing the church on the left. At the village green keep ahead along Sheephouse Lane, passing to the left of the Unitarian chapel.

The main buildings in the hamlet of Rivington are the two churches on either side of the green. Although on an ancient site, the parish church was rebuilt in the 16th century and restored in the Victorian era. The plain but dignified Unitarian chapel dates from 1703 and is one of the earliest Nonconformist chapels in Lancashire.

❷ At a public footpath sign, turn right along a path to two kissing gates. Go through the right-hand gate and follow a path across grassland to a broad track. Bear left along it to a car park by Hall Barn and Rivington Hall. Turn right along the side of the barn and keep ahead to pass through a gap beside a gate – there is a blue waymark here.

Mock ruins of Liverpool Castle with Rivington Pike in the distance.

There has been a building on the site of Rivington Hall since the Middle Ages but the present house, built around 1780, is an impressive example of Georgian architecture. For centuries it was the home of the Pilkington family, the former lords of the manor.

Continue through woodland. At a fork, take the left-hand track and at a crossways keep ahead through a kissing gate, in the direction of a 'Terraced Garden Trail' sign. Head gently uphill, go through another kissing gate and continue up through trees. Follow the path around a right bend and, at a fence corner, turn sharp left up steps to continue up through the former terraced gardens.

Turn left at a T-junction. Turn sharp right up steps and the path bends left. Turn right up some steps, pass under an arch and over a bridge. Go up more steps, pass beside a former summerhouse and climb steps to another T-junction. Turn left again, then turn right up steps. At a fork, take the right-hand path, passing under another arch and going up more steps. At the top, keep ahead up a final flight of steps. Turn left and pass beside a gate to reach the Pigeon Tower.

❸ Turn sharp right along a track. Bear left through a gate and head quite steeply up, via steps in places, to the tower on top of Rivington Pike.

The prominent landmark of Rivington Pike, one of the major landmarks of the western Pennines, rises to nearly 1,200 feet. From its summit, the superb all-round views take in the reservoirs at its base and the flat farmland of the West Lancashire plain beyond plus, in complete contrast, the bare and bleak Rivington and Anglezarke moors. The tower was built in 1773.

REFRESHMENTS

There is a café at Great House Barn, and a pub and restaurant at Hall Barn. The walk passes the Village Green Tearoom in Rivington which serves excellent breakfasts, morning coffee, lunches and afternoon teas (telephone: 01257 271669).

At the tower, turn right and head down across moorland to join a stony track. The track winds down to a gate. Go through and keep ahead to a T-junction. Go through a gate ahead, at a public bridleway sign, and continue downhill along a winding track, going through three gates.

❹ Soon after the third gate, turn right off the paved track onto a rough track to a fork and take the left-hand track, passing beside a gate. Follow this straight, tree-lined track for ½ mile. At a crossways in front of a gate, turn left along a track to a road. Cross over, keep ahead along a tarmac track and, where this track ends, continue along a path to a T-junction. Turn right to a crossways and turn left for a brief detour to the mock ruins of Liverpool Castle.

The castle, which occupies a fine position above Lower Rivington reservoir, is in fact a sham and represents the fantasy that many wealthy men at the time had of recreating a piece of the past. During the Victorian era the grounds of country houses became littered with imitation Greek and Roman temples and the mock ruins of medieval abbeys and castles. Lord Leverhulme was no different and had the castle constructed around 1900 as a picturesque feature of the park. The ruins are a replica of what the castle in the centre of Liverpool looked like around the time of its demolition.

❺ Return to the crossways and turn left – continuing in the same direction as before – along the right-hand edge of woodland fringing the shore of the reservoir. At a fork, take the left-hand path to continue along the edge of the trees and parallel to the reservoir – between a fence on the right and railings on the left. Look out for where you turn right to return to the starting point at Great House Barn.